R[illegible]DENING

7 SIMPLE ST[illegible] FOR CONTROLLING PESTS AND DISEASES, PRUNING, COMPANION PLANTING, DIFFERENT TYPES OF ROSES, PLANTING AND CARE, SOIL AND MORE

STEPHANIE STEPHENSON

Dedicated to my Dad who was a champion gardener, taught me everything I know about gardening, and is missed every day.

CONTENTS

FREE GIFT TO OUR READERS

In this Secret You Have in Your Home, you'll learn...

- How to make your garden flourish with ease
- How to control pests and weeds naturally
- Get sweeter tomatoes
- Treating fungus and mildew

Follow the link below to download your free guide.
https://stephaniestephenson.activehosted.com/f/1

BONUS

Join my Facebook Group where I talk about all things gardening and get a free copy of my Garden Planner.

https://www.facebook.com/groups/977894766376839

https://www.facebook.com/groups/977894766376839

ABOUT THE AUTHOR

Growing up, I was always surrounded by plants, especially roses. My father was a master gardener, and a majority of my childhood memories revolve around him tending to his roses in the garden. Gardening was the thing that brought me very close to my father because we would spend hours in the garden, learning about different kinds of roses and how to establish and graft them. Even though I was incredibly young at the time, the majority of my knowledge stems from the teachings of my father because I actually saw everything in action. It has been more than 20 years since he passed away, but I will always remember his kind words, his phenomenal brain, and his gentle disposition, as well as all the time we spent together in the garden. He has always been my role model, and even though he has passed, he has continued to accompany, encourage, and look after me from the beyond. He has always been my guardian angel.

After he passed, gardening was the only thing that continued to connect me to my father because whenever I was in the garden, I would go right back to my childhood. I could almost picture myself clinging to my father's leg while he gathered a bunch of roses to present to my mother. I threw myself into gardening, and it brought me such immense peace. It was because of these experiences that I decided to write a gardening book. I wanted to share that peace and tranquility I felt when I was among nature with the rest of the world. People underestimate the art of growing roses because, in a sense, they don't provide you with anything of value. However, roses are a symbolic representation, almost a manifestation, of love itself. So, what better way of spreading love than through your garden?

We might think of these memories as insignificant, but they hold great value for children because, when all is said and done, these minuscule moments will be the ones that will bring them joy. In the end, it was my time with my father that encouraged me to write this book, and because of that, it is very near and dear to my heart. I would like to sincerely thank anyone who has bought and read this book.

INTRODUCTION

"I'd rather have roses on my table than diamonds on my neck."

— EMMA GOLDMAN

John Keats once wrote, "A thing of beauty is a joy forever," and this is a statement that rings in people's minds, especially when they think about nature. Unfortunately, beauty is often considered to be fleeting, something that lasts for a small period of time; and after it is gone, a person or a thing's beauty becomes something that is easily forgettable. While this analogy might be fitting for a human, it doesn't really suit nature because even though flowers only bloom once, they leave a lasting impression, one that imprints in the mind of humans until the human is no more. There are many stunning elements of nature, but one of the most common and the most striking has and will always be roses.

Roses are infamous for many reasons, but the main reason for their popularity has to be their enduring legacy. Archaeologists have discovered rose fossils that date as far back as 35 million years, and they are the oldest species of plant to be grown as a decoration. Documents dating back to AD 50 have revealed that Ancient Romans grew roses on huge plantations and even in local hothouses to ensure that they had a year's supply. The roses were used for medicinal extracts, cooking ingredients, ornamentation, and even as decorations for furniture, people, and buildings. The fact that roses have basically been around since the beginning of civilization always surprises people, but what is even more shocking is that roses live for a really long time; the oldest living rose is over 1000 years old, and its presence has been documented since A.D. 815.

Roses are a symbolic representation of a wide variety of emotions, and many people love receiving them. And while receiving roses is very special, there is something otherworldly about cultivating and enjoying your own roses. Roses have a special place in people's hearts, but they are even more welcome when used to create visually appealing and delicious smelling gardens that improve the overall atmosphere of the home, providing homeowners with a special sort of comfort. Gardening often brings people together, and many people garden with their children or grandchildren in order to create memories that will last. Growing up, our family often gathered in the garden to plant and harvest different vegetables and flowers, and even after all these years, those memories still bring me immense joy. If gardening helps you create lasting memories, what better way to remember your loved ones than growing flowers that inherently represent love?

The problem is that, just like everything else, the thought of starting your own rose garden is often accompanied by a lot of fear. People are intimidated by the concept of growing their own plants, particularly roses, because they think that rose cultivation is only done by highly experienced gardeners, but that is far from the truth. Not only that, but the information about roses is scattered on the internet because there are so many different kinds of roses, and their health depends on the variety you choose and their hardiness. But this doesn't mean that you will have an incredibly hard time establishing rose plants. If you properly learn the steps of growing roses, they become some of the easiest plants to grow, and that is exactly what this book is about. It focuses on providing you with a step-by-step guide to help you get started with rose gardening. The steps are broken down into what is called the F.L.O.W.E.R.S. method, and each step is thoroughly explored in each chapter so that you get a lot of targeted information and don't have to go searching the web to find different techniques.

One thing that makes rose gardening difficult is the fact that they are very vulnerable to pests and diseases, despite being sturdy plants. However, pests and diseases aren't an issue if you know how to identify and treat the problems, which is why a whole chapter in this book focuses entirely on that. The process of starting the rose garden won't be easy, but once you figure everything out and the garden is established, all you will need to do is occasionally check on the garden and provide it with water and nutrients. So, let's put our fear aside and start digging in!

CHAPTER 1
THE ROSE ENCYCLOPEDIA

"If roses were not special weeds would not envy them."

— MATSHONA DHLIWAYO

I have always had a very close relationship with plants, particularly roses. My father had always been a big fan of growing plants, and around the time I was born, this passion turned towards growing roses. He always said that even though roses can't give you substance, they symbolize some of the most formidable powers in the world, one of which is love. In this chapter, you will learn about the ins and outs of rose gardening, particularly what, why, and how rose gardening came to be the sensation it is today, so you can start your journey towards becoming a rose gardener.

Roses have a very long and colorful history. According to the evidence provided by studying fossils, roses date back 35 million years. However, the cultivation of roses as garden ornaments started somewhere in China around 5,000 years ago. During the Roman period, roses took center stage, particularly in the Middle East, and they were used for their beauty, as medicine, for scents, and were even eaten. In the 15th century, roses became a symbol of war, and by the 17th century, the reverence for them had risen to the point that royalty used roses and rose water as barter or payments. Josephine, Napoleon's wife, established an extensive collection of roses in the Chateau de Malmaison, an estate located just outside Paris. It wasn't until the 18th century that cultivated roses were introduced in Europe, and most modern-day roses can be traced back to this exact ancestor (Our Rose Garden- History of Roses, n.d.).

But roses also have a little bit of dark history as they became part of the struggle within the Roman Empire when peasants were forced to grow roses instead of food, all to satisfy the needs of the upper class (*History of the Rose*, n.d.).

Early European roses were Rosa Gallica, which are native to Europe, and they are fragrant flowers that can be found in a variety of different shades. Officinalis is a stunning variety of pink rose that was introduced in France in the 13th century. A kind of Officinalis is also referred to as The Red Rose of Lancaster, Rosa Mundi, Versicolor, the Apothecary's Rose, and it seems to have originated in 1580. It was one of the most popular varieties of roses to exist in Europe.

THE ARRIVAL OF THE CHINA ROSE

Portland roses were overshadowed by the major developments made in China in the late 18th and 19th centuries, which resulted in the production of the China Rose. The parent flowers were introduced in 1752, and some hybrids followed them in 1792. The roses are what became the foundation of all hybrid varieties because they were first used to create Old Garden Roses that could reflower repeatedly, and then they helped create Modern Garden Roses (*History of the Rose*, n.d.).

WHAT IS A ROSE?

A rose is a flower that grows on a plant that is the part of the genus 'rosa.' There are over 100 species of roses that fall under this genus. Most roses are cultivated for their stunning flowers that range anywhere from white to maroon in color. The majority of rose species are native to Asia, which isn't surprising since they originated in China. Some roses are native to North America and some parts of Europe and northwest Africa. Roses that belong to different regions around the world tend to hybridize easily, giving rise to types with overlapping parental forms and making it much more difficult to determine the base species of the rose (Britannica, 2021).

Roses are climbing or trailing shrubs, and some species can even stand up on their own. The stem of the rose is riddled with thorns, and the leaves are oval-shaped and sharp-toothed. Wild roses only have five petals, but cultivated roses have double the number of petals (Britannica, 2021).

WHERE DO BLACK ROSES COME FROM?

Black roses almost seem like a myth, but they have existed in history for a long time and have a lot of symbolic significance. Not only are black roses extremely unique, but they are also extremely rare, and producing them is quite hard. However, black roses aren't actually black. They get their color from intense shades of red or purple, which is why it is impossible to find a purely black rose. But there are three varieties of roses that can replicate black roses since they produce the darkest flowers among all the varieties. The first variety is called Dark Jade, and the flowers of this plant turn a really dark shade during hotter months, but these plants are vulnerable to pests and diseases. The second variety is called the Black Baccara, and it produces the deepest shade you can naturally find, but because it is unscented it may not be appealing to a lot of people. The last option is Midnight Blue which does not produce black flowers but produces flowers in a very deep shade of purple and has a very strong scent (*The Black Rose: History, Meaning, and Symbolism – Venus ET Fleur*, 2020).

Roses have been symbolic throughout history, but black roses have always been a symbol of power and strength. Black roses have been particularly prominent in literature and movies, often symbolizing tragic love, danger, or even foreshadowing a tragedy. These roses were also used by the Sicilian mafia to send hidden messages, and if you were sent a black rose, it meant caution because death was approaching. Even now, black roses remain significant as a symbol for the gothic community (*The Black Rose: History, Meaning, and Symbolism – Venus ET Fleur*, 2020).

ROSE FACTS

If you are new to roses or just don't know much about them, here are some fun facts you should be aware of:

- ***Roses are one of the oldest flowers***

Roses have been ever-present in literature and music for centuries, and it is no wonder because archeologists have discovered rose fossils that date back 35 million years. An even more shocking fact is that the oldest living rose is about 1,000 years old, and this ancient rose grows on the walls of Hildesheim Cathedral located in Germany (Harmeyer, 2020).

- ***You can eat them***

Roses aren't just something to be kept in a vase. Rose petals are edible, and rose water is a common ingredient added to jellies or jams and is even used in Indian and Chinese cuisine. What most people are unaware of is the fact that rose plants can also produce a fruit which is referred to as rosehip. The fruit is dark orange, purple, red, and even black in color and is packed with vitamin C (Harmeyer, 2020).

- ***Rose fragrance is used in perfumes***

Roses are mostly known for their lovely aroma, which has become a very popular scent and is often used in perfumes, particularly for women. Rose oil, specifically, has become a very important ingredient in the perfume industry. However, this oil extraction process requires a huge number of roses; almost two thousand roses are needed to produce just one gram of oil (Harmeyer, 2020).

- ***Each rose color has a completely different meaning and interpretation***

Roses can be found in over 10 stunning colors, and each color has a very specific meaning. Red roses symbolize love and romance, and pink roses symbolize grace, elegance, and first love. Yellow roses, on the other hand, represent friendship, and the somber whites signify sympathy, which is why they are often found at funerals. White roses also symbolize purity, spirituality, and even innocence. Lastly, orange roses symbolize enthusiasm, so it might be a great idea to give these to someone who is graduating (Harmeyer, 2020).

- ***Rose is the national flower of the United States***

Roses became the national flower of the U.S. in 1986 when President Ronald Regan declared it the national emblem as he was standing in the famous White House Rose Garden (Harmeyer, 2020).

- ***Good quality and rare roses can be sold for millions of dollars***

Normal roses don't really cost much, but specially cultivated varieties can rack up quite a big price. The infamous rose breeder David Austin dedicated about 15 years of his life and spent 5 million dollars breeding a rare rose variety that he called Juliet. The Juliet sold for a whopping 15.8 million dollars in 2006 (Harmeyer, 2020).

- ***Symbol of the English War***

Roses were a symbol of the famous war called the 'Wars of the Roses' that lasted from 1455 to 1487 between different factions within England to gain control of the throne. A rose represented both factions: The House of York with a white rose and the House of Lancaster with a red rose (Kingsley, 2020).

- ***Roses are significant in Greek mythology***

As we have previously discussed, roses have always held significance in history and they are a prominent part of Greek mythology. They are often related to the Greek goddess of love, Aphrodite. It is said that the first red roses bloomed from her blood as she ran to her dying lover's side. This is why red roses symbolize everlasting love and devotion (Kingsley, 2020).

- ***Roses don't have thorns***

Even though we know the spiky things on roses as thorns, that is not their true name. People usually refer to them as prickles. This is because prickles don't stick straight out of the plant; instead, they are sickle-shaped, which helps them grab on to other plants as they grow over them (Kingsley, 2020).

- ***Roses have long lives***

A rose typically lives about 35 years, but if cared for properly, it can live for even longer (Kingsley, 2020).

- ***You can create rainbow roses***

You can create rainbow roses by taking a white rose, splitting its stem, and placing it in different colored dyes. The stem sucks up the color and turns the petals into the color you prefer (Kingsley, 2020).

- ***Roses have been to outer space***

A ROSE NAMED the Overnight Scentsation was sent into orbit on a Discover mission STS-95 in 1988. This rose became the first rose to be sent into outer space (Kingsley, 2020).

- ***Roses are state flowers***

New York, Georgia, Iowa, Washington, and North Dakota all have different rose varieties as their state flowers (Kingsley, 2020).

- ***Roses have sub-genre***

All rose varieties fall under one of these 4 genres: Rosa, Hesperrhodos, Hulthemia, and Platyrhodon (Kingsley, 2020).

- ***There are many different species of roses***

Roses don't just grow on plants as singular flowers; they can also be found as shrubs, groundcovers, trailers, and climbers (Kingsley, 2020).

PROS AND CONS OF ROSE GARDENS

Like everything, rose gardens also have their own pros and cons, and you need to be aware of both the advantages and drawbacks before starting a garden that is completely dedicated to roses.

Pros of Rose Gardening

- ***There is so much rose variety***

Unlike most flowers, roses don't come in consistent color and quantity. Rather, they have a lot of variety, and that is without a doubt one of their best qualities. Climbing roses can grow on walls or climb up fences up to 12 feet high; meanwhile, hybrid tea roses have long stems and produce large, fragrant blossoms. Roses can be found in pure whites, reds, pinks, and yellows and can even be speckled or marbled (Hartman, n.d.).

- ***Roses are very easy to grow***

While some rose varieties require a lot of money and effort to grow, common roses can be grown with relatively little effort. The best part is that roses can be grown in a variety of different soils as long as they get proper drainage. They don't need to be heavily fertilized and can tolerate several hours of direct sunlight. Too much sunlight can kill the flowers, but it will not damage the plant. Some roses are even repeated bloomers which means they can grow flowers repeatedly without any special attention (Hartman, n.d.).

- ***Roses give the growers some value***

Roses are a major source of income for people who grow them commercially, and florists traditionally sell them for special occasions such as birthdays, weddings, and Valentine's Day. The market prices for roses fluctuate just like any other commodity, and this fluctuation is based on the season, the quality and type of rose, and local supply and demand (Hartman, n.d.).

- ***Roses don't demand much from the environment***

Roses don't need a lot of water to grow, which reduces their impact on the environment. People who grow roses in gardens don't need to install sprinklers to water them since infrequent waterings work best, and some home growers even depend on rainfall to naturally water their roses (Hartman, n.d.).

- ***They can beautify your environment***

One of the best things about roses is that they turn any mediocre garden into an award-winning one. Their beauty in itself sets them apart from the rest, and when you take into account their amazing scent, they are unparalleled (Admin, 2020).

- ***Roses are rebloomers***

While some varieties only bloom once a year, most common roses tend to bloom on a 5-to-7-week cycle. After they bloom once, they will go through a rest period that spans a couple of weeks and then start the blooming process again (Will roses rebloom?, 2005).

Cons of Rose Gardening

- ***Roses can be messy***

Roses can be quite messy, especially if you are planting a bigger variety. You will get piles of fallen leaves and petals. And after the flower blooms, the petals will fall to the ground.

- ***They are susceptible to diseases***

The main disadvantage of roses is the fact that they are quite susceptible to diseases. And while some varieties are hardier than others, particular varieties can be incredibly sensitive. Fungus diseases are the most common, and you can quickly spot them by the black dots that appear on the leaves. To get rid of the diseases, you will need to ensure that your roses get proper circulation and spray the plants with a fungicide.

The second most common thing that attacks your roses is mildew, and the variety that is most susceptible is the Crimson Glory. So, if you are thinking about planting roses, you need to be prepared to deal with diseases.

- ***Some varieties of roses can fall apart***

While most people would think that bigger varieties would be better than smaller ones, that is not actually the case, and that is because the chance of you walking past a rose bush and getting hurt increases as the size of the bush increases. Often, gardens don't have enough space to accommodate bigger varieties, which means that gardeners have to constantly prune them to keep them under control. Take Heirloom Roses, for example, which can easily reach 8 feet in both height and width.

- ***Some species of roses can become very large***

Roses can be quite delicate, and some varieties can collapse under the weight of their leaves and flowers. While this usually happens during storms or rains, wind can also damage them. So, before you grow roses, you need to find tried and tested varieties or install support cages or trellis. (Viznyy, 2021)

In this chapter, we touched on the base of where roses originated. In the next chapter, we will explore the first step of the F.L.O.W.E.R.S. method, which is selecting roses.

CHAPTER 2
FIND THE ROSE THAT CALLS

"The gentle rose offers a powerful joy known only to the heart."

—ANDREW PACHOLYK

We know from the previous chapter that there are over 100 species of roses, and each of them not only has a different color and petal number, but their hardiness also changes. This means that if you wish to grow roses, you have plenty of variety to choose from, and you can match the hardiness of the plant to the area in which you live. While it is easy to verbally advise someone to pick out a rose, figuring out what kind of roses you want in your garden isn't as simple. Before we go forward with learning the tips and tricks for selecting the perfect roses for your garden, let's explore how and why roses have become the most sought-after flower around the world.

It isn't uncommon to encounter rows of roses as soon as you enter a flower shop. It is an incredibly stunning flower with a fragrant smell, and when all of that is combined with the fact that it can be found in a variety of different colors, roses become the perfect flower for almost any occasion. And while plenty of other flowers are just as pretty as roses, they have failed to reach the stature granted to these multi-petaled beauties. There are plenty of reasons why roses are popular, but the most important one is the fact that they are just as old as civilization itself; the earliest record of roses dates back to 2000 B.C. in what is known today as Iraq. The Chinese started cultivating the flower in 500 B.C., and since then, they have been used in medicine, perfumes, and even in food. So, it is easy to say that roses have been accompanying humanity longer than any other flower in existence, and it is no wonder people have formed such an attachment to them (How Roses Became the Most Popular Flower in History, n.d.).

Roses came to North America after it was colonized by the Europeans. With colonization, Europeans brought the popularity of rose gardens, especially among the elite. The oldest garden in North America is situated in Hartford, Connecticut, and dates back to 1904. It was created by Theodore Wirth, and he envisioned eight large archways, each with a different kind of rose variety. It has been over 100 years since the formation of this rose garden, and the eight archways still bloom every June (How Roses Became The Most Popular Flower in History, n.d.).

HOW DID RED ROSES BECOME A SYMBOL OF LOVE?

Nearly every culture and religion in the world associates red roses with passion, longing, and love. And while today we might not pay attention to why we associate roses with true love, there is a long and ancient history behind its presence in mainstream culture. Many myths and legends have made roses a part of cultural practices. One popular myth that paints roses as important is related to the ever-famous goddess of love, Aphrodite. Legend claims that roses, particularly red roses, grew from Aphrodite's tears and the blood of her human lover, Adonis, after he died in her arms. In another version of the same myth, Aphrodite nicked her foot on a white rose plant while running to her lover's side. The blood turns the white rose red, becoming the first-ever red rose in history, symbolizing Aphrodite's love. There are many other similar myths, but this one presents the clearest link behind the significance of the red rose in the floral industry (How Roses Became the Most Popular Flower in History, n.d.).

Over the years, roses have developed, and now there are more than 300 species and over 30,000 varieties. However, the most common are the long-stemmed roses that are often found in florist shops. Surprisingly, Ecuador is the third largest producer of cut flowers, and 75 percent of those are roses. The roses produced in Ecuador are recognized as some of the highest quality roses found in the world. This abundance is due to the growing areas that receive extremely long hours of sunlight, thanks to their location near the equator and their high altitude. Additionally, roses are grown in the mountains, which means that unless you plan to start your rose garden in the mountains of North America, you won't be able to achieve the same quality of roses. However, this doesn't mean that you won't be able to produce stunning and vibrant roses in your own garden.

STEPS FOR CHOOSING THE RIGHT ROSE

As previously stated, growing beautiful roses depends on choosing the right rose so that it matches the hardiness of your zone and is able to thrive in the soil that is present in your garden. Of course, you will have to add fertilizer to boost the nutrients every so often. So, here are a few steps you should follow when choosing a rose for your space.

STEP #1- Focus on the Appearance You Like

- ***Color***

Color is the most important aspect of roses, and if you plan to see them in your garden every day, you should choose a rose that is visually pleasing to you (Austin, 2021).

- ***Height***

The next thing you need to focus on is the height of your roses. As previously addressed, one major drawback of roses is that some species can spread quite far. And if you choose a rose that grows wider than your garden, not only will it look unattractive, but the plant might also find it difficult to thrive. So, consider the final height of the roses after they are fully grown before you buy the flower (Austin, 2021).

STEP #2- Go for Fragrances if that Is Important to You

- ***What do you like?***

Some people are allergic to strong scents, especially floral scents, so if that is an issue for you, you need to avoid roses that have excessive fragrance. Make sure to find roses that have a very subtle scent (Austin, 2021).

- ***What are you looking for?***

Choosing a rose plant ultimately depends on what appeals to you. So, you need to understand what kind of roses you are looking for to grow what will make you happy (Austin, 2021).

Step #3- How Many Roses Are You Looking to Grow?

- ***Consider the size of your garden***

When it comes to choosing roses, one thing is essential: considering the size of your garden. You want the flowers to be able to fit well and get adequate nutrients so that they can grow properly. Roses not only need adequate sun exposure, but they also need a lot of air, or they will start forming fungus (Austin, 2021).

- ***Consider your purpose***

The purpose of planting roses will also impact the kind of roses you choose. So, ask yourself why you are planting the roses. Do you wish to sell them, or are they just for aesthetic purposes? (Austin, 2021).

Step #4- Consider Your Location

- ***Check the climate in your area***

The climate of your particular region should constantly be on your mind while choosing rose plants since that will determine how well your roses will grow in your garden or if they will grow at all (Austin, 2021).

- ***Make sure it suits the rose plants***

If you live in a colder area and it snows for nearly six months per year, you need to choose a plant that can survive in that environment. Similarly, if you live in an area where it rains a lot, you need to find plants that are more resistant to diseases caused by excess water, such as black spots (Austin, 2021).

TYPES OF ROSES

Type #1: Hybrid Tea Rose

Hybrid tea roses are a cross of tea roses and hybrid perpetual, and these became the first modern rose type introduced in 1867. You can find them in a range of colors, and they are long-stemmed, which is what makes them a favorite among gardeners. Hybrid tea roses thrive in zones ranging from 5 to 9; they are bushy and can stand upright on their own and are about 2 to 3 feet wide. The best part of this rose is that they are repeat bloomers which means they bloom every year from late spring to fall. If you are looking for hybrid tea roses, try Peace, Double Delight, Fragrant Cloud, Just Joey, and Mister Lincoln. The only drawback of hybrid tea roses is that they are a little more sensitive compared to other roses and are more susceptible to pests and diseases (Loughrey, n.d.).

Type #2: The Miniature Rose

These plants are bred to be smaller, which means that they also produce smaller blooms. However, the name of these roses is quite deceiving, because while some varieties are extremely compact, others can grow as large as Floribundas. You can find these plants in both shrubs or climbing forms and they are great for smaller spaces, raised beds, rock gardens, stand-alone accents, and pathway edging. They thrive in the zones between 4 and 11. Their shrub forms grow to 1 to 3 feet and are about 2 feet wide, and their climbers can reach up to 8 feet tall. If you want to plant these, you should try Rainbow's End, Lavender Delight, Tiddly Winks, Hot Tamale, Angel Wings, and Gourmet Popcorn (Loughrey, n.d.).

Type #3: The Floribunda Rose

Floribunda roses were first developed back in the 1940s, and they are a hybrid of free-flowering nature and compact hybrid polyanthas. These roses have the same diverse color range as hybrid tea roses. They produce smaller flowers but cluster on bushy plants, which means that they are perfect for landscaping. They are easy to care for, and their hardiness ranges from 4 to 10, making them the perfect plant for beginners. They are bushy, which means that they can grow to about 5 feet tall and 3 to 4 feet wide at their full height. The best part is that they are repeat bloomers and produce blooms from early summer to fall. Try planting Cinco de Mayo, Iceberg, Amber Queen, Julia Child, Bonica, and Sunsprite (Loughrey, n.d.).

Type #4: Grandiflora Hybrid Roses

These plants are a shrub type that grow a little taller than typical shrubs, introduced in the 1950s. Grandiflora is a cross between hybrid tea roses and Floribundas and is characterized by clusters of 6 to 7 large blooms on one singular stem, making excellent cut flowers. They thrive in zones 5 to 9 and can grow up to 8 feet tall and 2 to 5 feet wide. Like other varieties, Grandiflora are also repeat bloomers. Try Dick Clark, Cherry Parfait, Mother of Pearl, Gold Medal, Octoberfest, and Tournament of Roses (Loughrey, n.d.).

Type #5: The Polyantha Rose

Polyantha was developed in the late 19th century, and they are well known for smaller flowers that grow in clusters of 1-to-2-inch blooms and without much fragrance. These are perfect for people who are sensitive to stronger scents. You can find them both as shrubs and climbing vines, and they are perfect for hedging or container plants because they are easy to take care of and virtually disease-free. They thrive in zones 4 to 10, and their shrub grows to be about 4 feet tall and wide, and the climbers can reach up to 10 feet in length and 6 feet in width. If you plan to plant these, you need to try China Doll, Cecile Brunner, The Fairy, Marie Pavie, and Perle d'Or (Loughrey, n.d.).

Type #6: The Climbing Rose

These roses don't really grow like vines, but they can be trained to grow on vertical cane or trellis. They are best used as screening or to provide some vertical interest to a landscape. Climbing roses are the most diverse out of the bunch and can survive in any hardiness between 2 and 10. They can grow up to 12 feet in length and become about 4 feet wide. Try planting Iceberg, Eden, William Baffin, Fourth of July, and Zephirine Droughin (Loughrey, n.d.).

Type #7: The Rambling Rose

Some people use the terms climbing and rambling roses interchangeably, but there is a slight difference between the two. Rambling roses only grow once during the season, while climbing roses can continue to bloom after their first bloom of the season. Ramblers also produce smaller roses compared to climbing roses, but they produce a lot more. Just like climbers, they can be tamed to follow trellises (A.D.A.M.S., 2021).

Type #8: The Ground Cover Rose

Ground cover roses are also called landscape roses, and they are often wider than they are tall; although, some can reach up to 3 feet in height. They bloom from spring to fall and could have either single or double blooms. They are fragrant but still resistant to pests and diseases, which is why they are great for first timers. Ground cover roses work exceptionally well on steep slopes. Flower Carpet is probably the most popular among the many different kinds and requires minimal maintenance (A.D.A.M.S., 2021).

Type #9: The Shrub

Shrub roses are designed to be low maintenance and hardy, and because there are so many shrubs rose varieties, you can get both old and modern roses. It's important to read the packaging before buying. Because there are so many types, shrub roses can be found in a lot of colors, flower sizes, and plant sizes. The best part is that they don't require deadheading even though they are profuse bloomers (A.D.A.M.S., 2021).

Type #10: The English Rose

The English Rose is also referred to as David Austin rose. They were named after the founder who created them by crossbreeding old gardens and modern roses back in the 1950s. The company is still around in Shropshire, England, and they still breed numerous varieties of roses. The company spends years growing roses and only select a few best hybrids to sell. There are more than 200 varieties of the English Rose, and many bloom repeatedly and are fragrant (A.D.A.M.S., 2021).

Type #11: The English Tree

English Tree roses thrive in zones 4 to 11 and prefer full or partial sunlight, depending on the variety. The best part is that they aren't overly picky about soil conditions. They are great along walkways, particularly when they are situated in pairs, and this is because they are incredibly fragrant and emit fruity or tea-like scents. They grow to be about 3 feet tall and need to be staked until they are fully developed. Like the English Rose, they can vary in petal and plant size (A.D.A.M.S., 2021).

PICKING THE BEST ROSES: THINGS TO CONSIDER

Even though we discussed quite a few kinds of roses, it can still be overwhelming to choose one, especially if you have no prior gardening experience. So, here are a few things that can help you decide which variety is the right one for you.

CONSIDERATION #1: Hardiness

The majority of roses thrive in warmer climates, particularly between U.S.D.A. hardiness zones 7 to 11. Some roses do have heat limitations and need to be planted in a specific range of hardiness so that they can thrive. On the other hand, some rose varieties are also sensitive to cold. So, if you only see a single zone listed on the rose plant or if there is no zone mentioned, then it is safe to assume that the plant can thrive in all zones up to 10 and 11 (8 Types of Roses: How to Choose Roses for Your Garden, 2022).

CONSIDERATION #2: Bloom Type

We have previously discussed that different varieties of roses can have a different number of petals, but they can also come in a variety of forms. Single roses often have four or fewer petals, semi-double roses have between 9 and 16 petals, double roses have 17 to 25 petals, and finally, full roses have somewhere between 26 and 40 petals. The roses can also be cupped, globular, quartered, flat, urn-shaped, pompon, and ruffled (8 Types of Roses: How to Choose Roses for Your Garden, 2022).

CONSIDERATION #3: Growth Habit

Different rose varieties can have different growth habits. Shrub varieties can be grown upright on their own, on a mounding, and even as ground cover. On the other hand, hybrid tea varieties can grow individual blooms on tall canes, miniature rose varieties are compact, and climbers and ramblers have woody stems that can be trained on a structure (8 Types of Roses: How to Choose Roses for Your Garden, 2022).

CONSIDERATION #4: Care Requirements

If you know that you won't be able to care for roses constantly, then you need to buy roses that are resistant to pests and diseases. This is because some roses are very sensitive to moisture, and if they aren't getting adequate airflow, they can quickly develop rot, mold, or fungus, which can destroy them. Rose bushes also need to be pruned; pruning is a delicate art and needs to be done with great concentration so that you avoid damaging the plant. But that doesn't mean that you can't prune your roses. Once you learn, you can start pruning your plants which will promote new growth, protect plants that are sensitive to diseases, and create the shape you desire. Roses also need to be fertilized every so often, and there are many different ways of going about it. Generally, it is fine to feed your plants 10-10-

10 fertilizers throughout every month when they are going through their growing season (8 Types of Roses: How to Choose Roses for Your Garden, 2022).

This chapter focused on introducing you to different kinds of roses and providing you with tips for choosing the best for your garden. The next chapter will focus more on the second step of the F.L.O.W.E.R.S. method: preparing the land for gardening.

CHAPTER 3
LAY OF THE LAND

"Roses do not bloom hurriedly; for beauty, like any masterpiece, takes time to blossom."

— MATSHONA DHLIWAYO

In the last chapter, we discussed different kinds of roses and their benefits, so now you will have a much easier time choosing roses for your garden. In this section, we will focus on the second step of the F.L.O.W.E.R.S. method, which involves surveying the land and preparing it for planting. As Rumi stated, "If your thought is a rose, you are a rose garden."

PICKING THE RIGHT SPOT

If you are trying to find the perfect spot for your roses, you need to keep quite a few things in mind. But before we can move on to talking about planting roses, let's talk about why finding the perfect location is important in the first place.

What Is the Importance of Finding the Right Location?

If you wish for your plants to thrive and remain healthy, then their location is one of the most important factors. If you place shade-loving plants in direct sunlight, not only will they stop growing but they will also be much more susceptible to pests and disease. Similarly, if you have a sun-loving plant, it will need at least 6 hours of continuous sunlight to grow properly. The problem is that sunlight or shade aren't the only factors that you have to consider; soil drainage is also a big issue. If a plant requires well-draining soil, you cannot get away with planting it inside predominantly clay soil because clay doesn't drain well at all. However, there are a few things you can do to improve the draining capability of your soil. One way of doing so is by digging a hole twice as wide as the plant requires and adding compost, manure, and peat moss before moving on to planting the rose. Some plants also prefer soils that retain water so figuring out the needs of your plants is essential (Location, Location, Location, n.d.).

I can’t tell you how often I have encountered people who are actually scared of growing roses because they think they are incredibly difficult to grow, but that is simply not true. All you need to do to be successful at growing roses is choose the right location. So, let’s discuss some important things that make any site an ideal place for roses (Griep, 2021).

Sun Exposure

A. A bush needs sun

Before choosing a spot, you need to figure out how much sunlight your plant will require each day. Generally, roses are sun-loving plants and need at least 6 hours of sunlight each day, but some roses can also work with partial sunlight, which means somewhere between 3 to 6 hours of sun exposure (Lofgren, 2021).

B. A location filled with sun is important

While it may seem tedious to try and find a spot with adequate sunlight, make sure to find an appropriate spot and don't try and make do with less sunlight than your plant needs. Not only will this result in unimpressive flowering further down the line, but it will also make your plants vulnerable to fungal diseases (Lofgren, 2021).

C. Direct sunlight can help fight off diseases

However, just picking the right spot that receives more than 6 hours of sunlight isn't enough; the timing of the exposure is equally important. Diseases like powdery mildew can settle on plants that have a lot of moisture on the foliage in the morning. So, in order to counter this, you need to choose a spot that receives those 6 hours of sunlight during the morning so that it dries off the dew (Lofgren, 2021).

The Amount of Space

- ***An ideal location has a lot of space***

If you look at great rose gardens that exist around the world, you will be able to instantly see that they have wide-open spaces without a lot of shade and crowding from other bushes, trees, or buildings. Usually, the ground is flat or on a slight incline, and because they aren't crammed together, the plants have a lot of space for circulation. So, an ideal location should have a lot of space (Lofgren, 2021).

- ***Roses need a good amount of space to grow***

The international rose test garden has the ideal rose plantation since none of the fir trees are blocking light and air, and each plant has a good amount of space, so they aren't crowded by other kinds of roses or other plant varieties. Roses need a lot of space in order to thrive, so you will need to provide them with the right kind of conditions. This includes planting away from trees and large bushes and giving them room between structures like fences and buildings (Lofgren, 2021).

It is a good idea to plant shrub roses diagonally or randomly rather than in a singular line so that they can have plenty of space on all sides. And even though sunlight is an important part, you can still grow ground cover and climbing roses; all you need to do is find a variety that can handle those kinds of conditions. You can even pair your roses with other kinds of plants. Just make sure that the type of plants you choose are shorter than the roses so that they don't crowd them. You should also consider that the roses you plant will grow much bigger than you think, and even though you may think that you can make a bush that requires 8 feet of space fit inside a 7-foot space, it is never a good idea (Lofgren, 2021).

- ***They won't thrive in crowded places***

Roses never do well if they are pruned shorter than they are meant to be, and the first thing that is usually affected is the flowering. If you still go through with it, you will either be extremely frustrated with the growth of your flowers or frustrated by how it snags at you while you are passing by. So, if you wish to avoid this problem, research, and learn how big your selected variety will get (Lofgren, 2021).

Protection

- ***Consider the winds***

It is essential that your plants have an ample amount of space, but at the same time, vast spaces can leave the plants vulnerable to wind. Strong wind can accidentally cause the plant to shift, which can weaken it, affecting its growth. Wind can also cause the plants to dry out quicker than normal, which means that you will need to water them more often. Therefore, you need to give them space but still plant them near a structure so that they will be protected from rough winds. This seems like a challenging situation, but it is much easier than it looks (Lofgren, 2021).

- ***Watch for environmental hazards***

Aside from the wind, your plants could also be vulnerable to storms, snow, and rain, and planting them near your home or wall can help protect them. So long as they are getting plenty of sunlight and air circulation, you can comfortably grow roses (Lofgren, 2021).

Preparing the Soil

After you find the perfect spot to plant your roses, you can start getting the soil ready for planting. Of course, every garden has a different kind of soil, so if you want to successfully grow your roses, you might need to add some elements to bring your soil up to standards. Plus, figuring out the kind of soil you have is the most important part because you can only fix it if you know what it needs exactly.

WHAT IS THE IMPORTANCE OF HEALTHY SOIL?

Healthy soil is the foundation of our food system, and the medium in which all our food-producing plants are grown. Therefore, healthy soil is needed to grow healthy produce so that it can also provide essential nutrients to humans and animals. In a sense, soil quality is directly linked to the quality and quantity of food. Soil not only supplies plants with essential nutrients but also acts as a buffer and protects them from excess water, harsh winds, and drastic temperature fluctuations (Healthy soils are the basis for healthy food production, 2015).

Healthy soil is considered to be alive because of the rich ecosystem that exists within its folds. It is teeming with microscopic organisms as well as other organisms that perform vital functions such as covering up the decaying and dead matter, cycling nutrients, controlling diseases, improving soil structure, improving water-retaining capacity, and improving crop production, among many other things (Healthy soils are the basis for healthy food production, 2015).

WHY IS ORGANIC MATTER IMPORTANT?

The organic matter that exists in soil is a product of on-site biological decomposition of some kind, and it affects the overall chemical and physical properties of the soil as well as its overall health. The composition of organic matter and its breakdown rate affects the structure of the soil and its porosity. It also affects the water infiltration rate, moisture-retaining capacity of the soil, diversity and the biological activity of the soil organisms, and the availability of plant nutrients. The nutrient exchanges that happen between organic matter, water, and soil are essential for soil fertility and need to be maintained for sustainable production purposes. When you keep planting in soil without reimbursing it for lost nutrients, the nutrient cycle breaks down, which results in declining soil conditions and, ultimately, a collapsed ecosystem (Healthy soils are the basis for healthy food production, 2015).

TYPES OF SOIL

While there are many other kinds of soils, these are the most common ones, so let's explore some of them.

- **Clay**

Clay soils are heavier than other types because they are very high in nutrients. They also remain wet and cold during winters and dry out during the summer. Over 25 percent of these soils are made up of clay, and because there are a lot of spaces between clay particles, clay soils are able to retain large amounts of water. However, clay soils can be quite difficult for gardeners to work with because they take longer to drain and warm up very slowly in the summer (Soil Types, n.d.).

- **Sandy**

Sandy soils are light, dry, acidic, and warm, and traditionally they are much lower in nutrients than other soils. They are considered to be lighter since they have a high proportion of sand and very little clay, which tends to be heavier. They drain water quickly and are easy to work with, but they have their own drawbacks as they tend to dry out quickly and lose nutrients to rain. However, elements can be added to sandy soils, and you can add organic matter to help give plants the additional boost they need to thrive (Soil Types, n.d.).

- **Planting Mix**

When you are planting a rose bush or any kind of tree, then you will need to improve the soil quality in the planting hole. Organic planting mix consists of aged arbor fines, peat moss, and rice hulls which can become a great supplement for your soils. However, you need to keep in mind that the planting mix is not a soil replacement but rather a soil amendment (Best Garden Soil to Buy For Your Plants, 2019).

- **Potting Mix**

PLANTS THAT ARE GROWING inside a pot or in a raised bed have completely different requirements from the plants that are growing inside the ground. This is why you must use a potting mix for your potted plants and raised beds, and not planting or organic planting mix (Best Garden Soil to Buy for Your Plants, 2019).

- **Silt**

Silt soils are not only light, but they retain moisture extremely well. Plus, they have very high fertility, and because their particles are medium-sized, they drain well and retain moisture at the same time. However, because the particles are fine, the soil can easily get compacted and wash away with rain. But if you add organic matter, the particles can form into more stable clumps (Soil Types, n.d.).

- **Peat**

Peat soil is high in organic matter and retains large amounts of moisture. These kinds of soils are rarely found in gardens and are often added to provide an optimum soil base for planting (Soil Types, n.d.).

- **Chalk**

Chalky soils can be both heavy and light, but one thing is for certain: they always contain high amounts of calcium carbonate, which is why they are highly alkaline. Because they are alkaline, they will not support the growth of plants that require acidic soils to thrive. If your already chalky soil has white lumps, then you must choose plants that prefer alkaline soils (Soil Types, n.d.).

- **Loam**

Loamy soils are a mixture of silt, sand, and clay, and people combine them together to avoid the negative effects of each type of soil independently. Loam is fertile, easy to work with, and has exceptional drainage, and because it is the perfect balance of all soil types, it's considered the best type of soil to plant in. But just like other soils, loamy soils also benefit from additional organic matter (Soil Types, n.d.).

ROSE SOIL PH

Now that we have become well acquainted with different kinds of soils, let's talk a little more about the ideal soil for roses.

- ***The optimum pH is 6.5***

Is it too acidic or too alkaline?

The pH is the measurement that indicates the acidity or alkalinity of the soil. The pH affects how the roses access nutrients from the soil, so it is something that you should pay attention to. If the pH is off, then your roses won't grow no matter how much you care for them. Lucky for you, most roses prefer a soil pH that is similar to ordinary garden soil, which is slightly acidic to neutral (between 6.0 to 7.0) (IANNOTTI, 2021).

- ***How to lower the pH?***

You can easily find soil tests to figure out the pH of your soil. If your pH is outside the range, you can easily make amendments before planting, but they can also be made after planting. If your soil is extremely alkaline or acidic, then it might be a good idea to grow your roses inside a container, because adjusting the pH requires continuous effort and it isn't a one-time fix. You can reduce the pH of soil by adding sulfur, aluminum sulfate, and sulfuric acid (IANNOTTI, 2021).

PREPARING THE SOIL FOR ROSES

All plants have different types of requirements, and if you want your plants to thrive, you need to learn their specific needs so that you can better cater to them. Typically, soil preparation should start at least a couple of months in advance, so the soil has at least 4 to 6 weeks to settle in and develop beneficial microbes and bacteria. Roses are pretty easy to work with, and they can adapt to almost any kind of soil so long as it's not light and sandy. Water retention is the biggest problem when it comes to roses, but this can be easily fixed if by adding some amendments. So, let's look at some of the important aspects of soil preparation so that you can be better prepared to make amendments to your soil (Soil Preparation, n.d.).

- **Healthy Microorganisms**

Once you figure out the pH of the soil, you need to start thinking about the beneficial microorganisms that exist within the soil. They are essential for any kind of plant because they break down organic matter so that plants have an easier time taking up the nutrients. Healthy microorganisms also eliminate pathogens from within the soil using a process called competitive exclusion. During this process, good microbes multiply quicker than bad microbes and, in some situations, even feed on them. Keeping the microbes happy involves introducing amendments into the soil and enriching it (Griep, 2021).

- **Enriching the Soil**

Compost, alfalfa meal, kelp meal, and peat moss all make great amendments. You can also buy bagged organic compost at the market, but before you buy it, just make sure to read the back to check what is inside. You can also easily make your own compost at home, and local gardening stores also carry supplies that can help you get started (Griep, 2021).

- ***Alfalfa Meal***

This is one of the best ways to give your plants some nitrogen, not to mention that it is well-balanced with potassium and phosphorus. It is also abundant in Triacontanol, which is a growth stimulant and a regulator (Griep, 2021).

- ***Kelp Meal***

This is a slow-release potassium supplement and provides plants with over 70 chelated trace minerals, growth-producing hormones, vitamins, and amino acids (Griep, 2021).

- ***Compost***

Compost is basically decomposed organic matter that improves the overall quality of the soil and increases microorganism activity (Griep, 2021).

- ***Mulch***

Mulch is basically a bunch of organic matter that is put on top of the soil and around the plants to keep the roots cool, retain moisture, and suppress weeds. People usually choose organic materials for mulching because it breaks down over time and continues to provide the soil with nutrients. If you use non-organic mulch, you might have to do the hard work and remove all of it later when your plants no longer require mulching. Organic mulch includes compost, leaf mold, and wood bark (IANNOTTI, 2021).

ORGANIC MATTER

If you are planning on using compost for your soil, then you need to know a little bit more about the different kinds available on the market or compost that you can create at home. So, let's discuss some common composting options available for home gardeners.

- ***Well-rotted compost***

Well-rotted compost is basically traditional compost that is made from organic material but is rotted enough that the whole thing looks like a bunch of healthy, brown soil. This kind of compost has been aged for quite a bit and is full of beneficial bacteria, microbes, and nutrients, giving your plants that boost they need to thrive. This compost is often entirely made up of vegan ingredients, which is great because it reduces agricultural waste. It is also odorless, which is amazing if you are planning on adding it to plants in your garden or inside your home. The only drawback is that it is a little difficult to achieve a 30:1 nitrogen to carbon ratio. Additionally, it takes a long time for this compost to get ready; in most situations, it can take up to 6 months (6 Types of Compost You Should Know, 2020).

- ***Worm castings***

Worm castings also fall under a type of compost which is called Vermicomposting. During the process of producing this compost, worms are encouraged to feast upon organic material so that they can digest it and produce excrement called casting. Vermicompost is full of nutrients which is particularly beneficial for potted plants. You can easily create this kind of compost at home; it increases water retention and enhances plant growth as well as crop yield. The problem is that worms are sensitive to extreme temperatures, direct sunlight, citrus fruits, dairy products, and meat, which means you must be careful about what you add to the compost and manage the temperature of the composting bin (6 Types of Compost You Should Know, 2020).

- ***Mushroom compost***

Mushroom compost is rich in nutrients, and its primary purpose is to grow mushrooms commercially. The organic materials that are used to make mushroom compost vary depending on the manufacturer, but typically, the compost is made up of horse or chicken manure, peat, gypsum, rye straw, wheat, grape clippings, and cottonseed meal. It increases water retention and adds a lot of nutrients to the soil. Additionally, it is a great way to reduce waste created by agriculture in an eco-friendly way. The only drawback is that mushroom compost contains a high content of soluble salts, which can have a negative effect on young and salt-sensitive plants and could also kill germinating seeds (6 Types of Compost You Should Know, 2020).

- ***Old manure***

Manure can be of two types: animal feces and green manure. Both have their own advantages and are popular choices among home gardeners. It is low cost, reduces agricultural waste, kills parasites, improves water retention, adds nitrogen to the soil, and aerates the soil. However, the manure made from animal feces can be inconvenient because it has a very pungent smell. Additionally, nutrients can also vary depending on what the animals have been fed, so it might be a good idea to read the back of the bag to crosscheck the nutrient content (6 Types of Compost You Should Know, 2020).

One really good way of figuring out if your soil is healthy without having to do a bunch of tests is by checking for good bugs, particularly earthworms. Earthworms actually help introduce air into the soil and keep it nice and fluffy. They also ensure that all biological processes remain in good shape and keep running like a well-oiled machine (Griep, 2021).

CONTAINERS

You don't have to get discouraged if you don't have a lot of space in your garden or don't have a garden at all, because you can still plant roses through container gardening. Most people aren't aware of container gardens, so let's explore them in detail.

What Is Container Gardening?

Container gardening is basically where gardeners grow plants inside specific containers rather them growing them in the ground. There can be many reasons for choosing container gardening, but primarily, container gardening comes in handy in urban areas where personal gardens are scarce. People who have temperamental or sandy soil also tend to choose container gardening since you can fully control and customize the kind of nutrients your plants receive. The best part of container gardening is that they are mobile and space-efficient, so you can arrange them anywhere you like. Plus, you can utilize old containers and upcycle them to plant new trees. Container gardens not only help you cut down your gardening budget, but they are also environmentally friendly. There is no shortage of what you can grow inside a container garden, but the most popular thing to grow are berries and flowers, like roses, because they are fairly low maintenance (Container Gardening, n.d.).

You don't need to worry too much about the kinds of containers that will be able to harbor your plants because almost any container that can hold soil can also hold your plants. The best thing you can do is reuse older containers that you have lying around the house because you won't have to pay for them, and it will be eco-friendly. If you are looking for new containers, you can always hit up the thrift stores because they have plenty of options that are much more affordable (Container Gardening, n.d.).

Pros of Container Gardening

Container gardens have a lot of benefits, so let's discuss some of them.

- ***Garden anywhere***

The best thing about container gardens is that you can virtually plant anywhere, be it an apartment, condo, or any kind of urban housing that doesn't come equipped with an outdoor garden. This opens a lot of doors for people who wish to garden to reduce their carbon footprint and environmental impact but are unable to because they don't have direct access to a backyard (Pointdexter, n.d.).

- ***Easier to raise plants***

Because the soil in pots and containers is less compacted and can be easily aerated, it is much easier to raise plants, particularly root crops. (Pointdexter, n.d.)

- ***Grow larger plants***

If you think that pots won't be able to handle bigger plants, you are absolutely wrong! You can easily utilize bigger containers in order to grow plants that are a little bigger in size, like corn (Pointdexter, n.d.).

- ***Pots can be moved around***

If you are wondering what exactly makes container gardening better than traditional gardening, the first thing that comes to mind is the fact that they are highly portable. So, even if one spot doesn't get continuous sunlight throughout the day, you can easily pick up the container and move it so that it is getting the sunlight it needs to survive. This way, you won't have to spend tons of time finding the perfect spot to plant your plants or roses (Pointdexter, n.d.).

- ***Fewer weeds***

Another benefit of container gardens is fewer weeds. This is because the containers that are harboring the plants are filled with potting soil, which has never been contaminated with weeds. This means that even if your plants somehow get contaminated with weeds, their quantity will be few and far between (Pointdexter, n.d.).

- ***Good protection from pests***

Most container plants are kept inside the house, so not only are you constantly viewing them 24/7, but they are also protected from the elements, which means that they are less vulnerable to pests. And because container plants are often spread around the space instead of being in one singular spot, it is easier to control the spread of disease (Pointdexter, n.d.).

IN-GROUND GARDENING

If you are lucky enough to have your own garden space or backyard, then you can consider choosing a more traditional kind of gardening. But what exactly is in-ground gardening? Let's learn a little bit more about it and its advantages.

What is in-ground gardening?

In-ground gardening is exactly what it sounds like. It is a piece of earth that has been plowed and tilled until it is suitable for plantation. The earth must be plowed because it makes it much easier for plants to form stronger roots if there are no soil clumps. The soil also needs to be amended because, often, typical garden soil is missing the essential nutrients that are necessary for plant growth. And because garden soil has had exposure to a lot of different plants, there is a possibility that you might have to weed it (Pointdexter, n.d.).

Pros of In-Ground Gardening

- ***Style the garden however you want***

When you have a flat piece of earth, you can grow plants however you like without having to worry about whether they will fit or not. The majority of people who own houses with backyards have enough space to easily grow at least a dozen different plants. In-ground gardening also offers more planting space, which is essential when planting on odd-shaped areas of your property (Pointdexter, n.d.).

- ***Grow a large number of roses***

Often when you have container gardens, you can only plant one or two plants per pot, but that isn't an issue with in-ground gardens because they offer enough space to easily plant a large number of roses. And while you can have a bigger harvest, you won't have to compromise on the quality (Pointdexter, n.d.).

- ***You don't have to water often***

The best thing about in-ground gardening is definitely the fact that you don't have to water often, especially if you have thoroughly saturated the soil (Pointdexter, n.d.).

- ***Cost-effective***

When you are doing container gardening or raised bed gardening, you have to invest a lot of money upfront, especially if you don't want to thrift or reuse older materials. Even if you save a bit of money, you will have to spend money on potting soil and amendments because potted plants have a lot more requirements since they aren't getting the nutrients directly from the ground. When you are in-ground gardening, you already have soil, and it only needs to be amended occasionally, which means that you save a lot of money, especially in the beginning (Pointdexter, n.d.) (Gibson, n.d.).

- ***It is well-draining***

If you have rich, healthy, and well-draining soil, then you don't have to spend money or go through the trouble of building raised beds; you can plant directly in the ground. Most garden soils are well-draining because the water gets absorbed into different parts of the soil, so it doesn't get mushy like potting soil. All you will need to do to fix your garden soil is amend it with fertilizer and add some compost between growing seasons (Gibson, n.d.).

- ***Suitable for large scale gardening***

If you are planning to grow a lot of crops, then in-ground gardening would be much more suitable for you. This is because you can easily use bigger machinery and plowing devices instead of manually doing the work since using machine-operated devices isn't possible with raised beds or container gardens (Gibson, n.d.).

RAISED BED GARDENS

Raised bed gardens have a lot of benefits, especially if you are looking for something temporary. But before you can choose any of the three options for planting, let's explore raised beds in detail.

What Exactly Are Raised Beds?

Raised garden beds can be best described as huge containers with soil that function as the base for growing plants. Raised beds are also referred to as garden boxes or planter boxes, and they are primarily built using wood, but they can also be made using stone, bricks, concrete, lumber, logs, fabric, galvanized metal, or any other material that is sturdy enough to bear the weight of the soil and plants. The best thing about raised garden beds is that you are able to enjoy the benefits of a traditional garden without having to deal with temperamental soil and invasive weeds (Cat, 2020).

Generally, your raised bed sits on top of existing garden soil and can be anywhere from a few inches to a few feet in height. Typically, each raised bed has plenty of room on the outside, so you can easily go around the box without accidentally clumping up the soil. This means that your soil will stay light and fluffy for a long time, which is essential since the roots grow best if there is easy access to air and water. The best thing about raised beds is that you can build your own beds depending on what kind of size and shape you like. The thing that often turns people off from investing in raised beds is the building aspect, but if you don't want to build your own, you can simply buy the raised bed kits, which are much easier to construct since they come with pre-cut pieces (What Is a Raised Bed, Anyway?, n.d.).

Whatever you choose to make the raised bed, it should be narrow enough that you are easily able to reach the middle of the bed from all sides. The beds can be as long as you want, and you can also change the depth of the bed depending on what kind of plants you are looking to grow. For instance, deep-rooted plants like mini trees and tomatoes need a lot more soil to be able to grow properly as compared to plants like lettuce and pansies (What Is a Raised Bed, Anyway?, n.d.).

Raised beds also don't have a bottom, but the majority of them are covered with mesh made of metal. This can help limit the issues that happen with wildlife, weeds, and other kinds of pests. Native soil or topsoil should never be used inside raised beds because it is really heavy. Instead, beds should be filled with bagged soil which is much lighter and doesn't burden the structure of the raised bed (What Is a Raised Bed, Anyway?, n.d.).

The Pros of Raised-Bed Gardening

There are a lot of benefits of raised beds, so let's discuss some of them.

- ***Plant earlier***

Because raised beds have exceptional soil drainage, they dry out faster than traditional gardens, which means that they warm up faster and are ready for planting much earlier in the season. Many plants are also able to overwinter inside raised beds which isn't usually possible otherwise. However, the majority of this depends on the kind of soil that exists within your garden. If the soil remains untilled and enriched with compost, the soil can self-regulate with more precision than disturbed and nutrient-deficient soil (Faires, 2017).

- ***Protects the plants***

Raised beds keep pests and rodents away from plants, which means that they will be constantly protected from outside threats. Just make sure to cover the bottom of the raised bed with hardware cloth, chicken wire, or any other kind of base, making sure that whatever you choose has plenty of holes for drainage. This will prevent any gropers and other critters from entering the bed (Gibson, n.d.).

- ***Grow a variety of roses***

Raised beds have plenty of space which allows you to grow a variety of different plants, particularly roses. The best part is that you don't have to limit yourself to just roses; you can grow a lot of different types of plants alongside them because almost all kinds of plants can be cultivated inside raised beds (Gibson, n.d.).

- ***Fewer weeds***

You won't have to be concerned about weeds and other invasive plants messing with your roses because if you are planting inside a raised bed; the chances of weeds finding their way inside are very slim.

- ***More control***

Raised beds allow you to add your own soil, create your own container, and personalize a bunch of other things, which means that you have a lot of control over your plants. This wouldn't have been possible if you chose to go the traditional route and plant in-ground.

- ***You won't have to till the soil***

A raised bed is the best kind of investment because once it is set up, you essentially have little or no work to do in order to maintain it. You won't have to till the ground every season; instead, you will only add soil and amendments on top of the soil. Any amendments or compost goes directly into the top few inches of the bed, and the soil is automatically tilled as the worms and roots push through the soil to get the nutrients they need. Tilling that is done by human hands often breaks up the organic connections and natural soil structures that are necessary for soil health (Faires, 2017).

- ***Great for people with back problems***

If you are someone who struggles with back problems or you have some disabilities that prevent you from doing relaxing activities like gardening, then raised gardens are the best option for you. This is because you won't have to bend over at all when tending to your gardens (Faires, 2017).

In this chapter, we went into great detail about various kinds of soil, the best pH for roses, different gardening options, and many other things. In the next chapter, we will be focusing on the third step of the F.L.O.W.E.R.S. method- how to plant a rose.

CHAPTER 4
OVER AND UNDER THE ROSE

"The rose is a rose from the time it is a seed to the time it dies. Within it, at all times, it contains its whole potential. It seems to be constantly in the process of change: Yet at each state, at each moment, it is perfectly all right as it is."

— PAULO COELHO

Roses are well-loved all over the world, and that much is evident from all the history we have previously delved into. There are many nations that celebrate roses and have gardens that are often home to a huge variety of roses. But did you know that the biggest rose garden doesn't exist in the west, but rather in the east? The world's largest rose garden is situated in Central Japan, located in Kani City in the Gifu Prefecture. This rose garden has more than 7,000 different rose varieties and is home to over 30,000 rose bushes. A festival is held each year to celebrate the roses, which also gives the locals an opportunity to view the garden in full bloom. You can reach the rose festival by bus which is present to make it easier to get to the venue.

In the last few chapters, we have gone into detail about the background as well as what roses require in order to thrive. In this chapter, we will move on to talking about the best time to plant roses and how exactly to plant them so that you can make the most out of your roses.

PLANT TIMING

Many inexperienced gardeners may think that summer is the best time to plant anything; after all, the majority of the growing happens during summer, but that's not necessarily the case. While the majority of plants prefer being planted in the spring, some plants like shrubs and perennials should be planted in the fall. There are quite a few things that determine the perfect time for plantation. But if there are so many factors, how exactly can you figure out the perfect time for planting your roses? Well, there are a few tips that can help you narrow down when your roses should be planted, so let's discuss some of them (Grunert, n.d.).

Timing Tips

Tip #1: Your zone determines the best time

Before you can even think about planting your roses or bare roots, you need to check the Hardiness Zone of your area and find the date for the last frost. After you find that out, you can easily follow the zone guidelines and proceed with planting your roses. In most hardiness zones, the best time to plant any rose plant is during early spring, which often falls between late February and April (Grunert, n.d.).

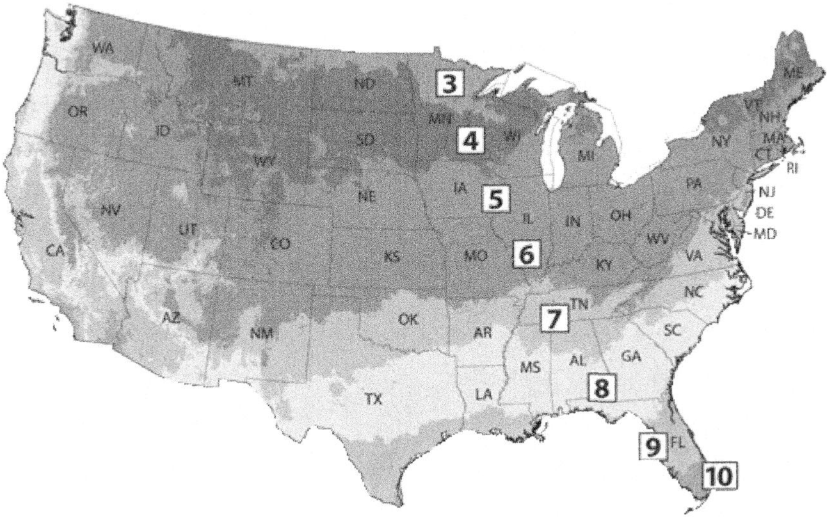

Tip #2: Roses should be planted after the first frost date has passed

You can use the U.S.D.A. Hardiness Zone map to make sure that you have the right zone information. The zones are listed between 1 to 13, with zone 3 being the coldest zone that can support roses. If you fall between zones 10 to 13, then you might not have enough cold for Gallica and Alba roses to bloom, so please check your local nursery before planting anything. This is because local nurseries can give you the most accurate information surrounding hardiness zones (Grunert, n.d.).

Tip #3: The soil should be warmed up

You should only plant your roses after the danger of frost has passed. The soil should be warmed and easy to work with; otherwise, it will be impossible for you to be able to dig into the frozen ground. And even if you manage, your roses won't take root (Grunert, n.d.).

Tip #4: Soil that is too frozen, sopping wet, or muddy won't work

If you are planning on planting in frozen or sopping wet soil, then you can't plant your roses into the round. The wet soil will prevent the plant from taking root, and even if the plant does take root, the wet soil may cause the plant to develop mold (Grunert, n.d.).

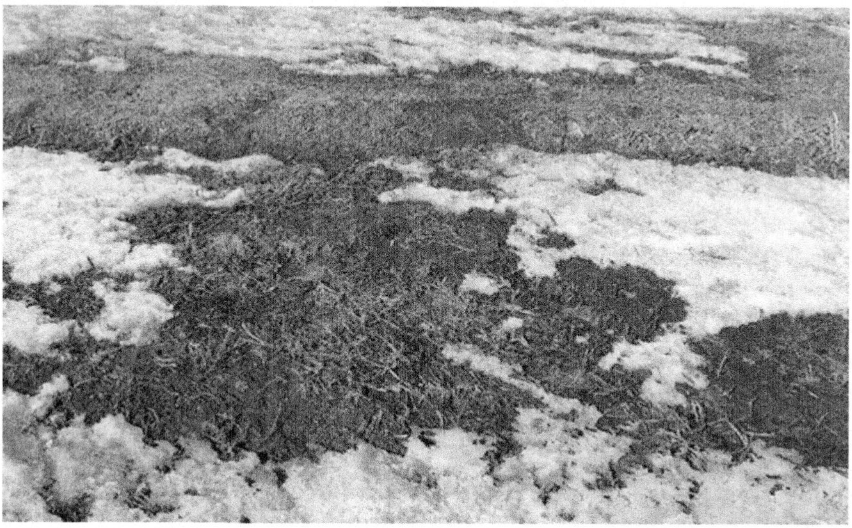

Tip #5: Wait until the soil is dry enough

If you have encountered wet soil, then all you need to do is wait until it is dry enough before planting. This will ensure that your roses get a healthy and happy environment that promotes growth (Grunert, n.d.).

What Is the Best Time to Plant Roses?

You can find most rose plants in two forms: inside containers and bare-root roses. Both have their own benefits, but they are quite different. Container roses are great for people who are new to gardening since they are not only easy to plant, but also establish themselves fairly quickly. You can easily find container roses in your local nursery through the growing seasons, and when you buy locally, you will be able to plant when the climate conditions are ideal. Bare-root roses, on the other hand, are great if you are looking for a variety of different roses. In addition to that, bare-root roses are economical, and you can easily order them online. However, bare-root roses can cause a little bit of a problem since they need to soak in water overnight before plantation, and they also require additional care after planting (Balogh, 2020).

Now that you have learned a little bit more about the kinds of plants you can source through the seasons, let's talk about the ideal time to plant roses.

- ***Roses are best planted in spring or fall***

Roses should be planted in spring or, most prominently, after the last frost date. However, they can also be planted in the fall, particularly six weeks before the first frost in your area (Balogh, 2020).

- ***Planting early gives the roots time to accumulate***

Planting early will give the roots enough time to establish before they have to grow dormant over winter. Bare-root roses are typically only available in early spring, and they should be planted immediately. But if you are buying roses in containers, then you will have more flexibility with the planting time (Balogh, 2020).

HOW TO PLANT?

When you buy any plant, it won't look like the garden version you often see in nurseries or online. Rather, it will look incredibly ugly and come in a plastic bag that is full of sawdust and peat moss. You may even find the plants as bare roots, which resemble a thorny stick that almost looks dead. While these roses aren't as fragile as one might think, a little extra effort put in during planting can help you create a healthier plant that produces more blooms. So, let's discuss some steps you need to take to prepare to plant your roses (IANNOTTI, 2021).

Step #1: Prepare the Hole

- ***Wider but equal in depth to the root ball***

Dig a hole that is slightly wider but just as deep as your root ball. This means your hole will be about 15 to 18 inches deep by 18 to 24 inches wide (IANNOTTI, 2021).

- ***Try mixing a handful of bone meal or superphosphate***

Mix a handful of superphosphate and bone meal in the soil you take out of the ground and save it so that you can refill the hole with the same soil. This will help the rose bush to acclimate to its new home. Don't add any amendments during plantation time. Any amendments to the soil should have been made weeks in advance. If you haven't added any organic compost or amendments, you can do it once the roots take hold and start producing new growth (IANNOTTI, 2021).

- ***Mix in some compost or organic matter***

When you remove some soil to dig the hole, keep the soil that you have dug up. This is because you can add additional nutrients, such as organic compost and manure, to the soil by mixing the soil with these amendments. This is a great way to reintroduce nutrients into the soil without shocking the plant (IANNOTTI, 2021).

Step #2: Prepare the Rose

- ***Remove it from the container***

If your roses came in a container, take them out of it. You might also need to wiggle the plants a little bit in order to get them out of the pot. However, while doing this, ensure you aren't yanking out the plant too roughly. Also, make sure to wear a pair of gardening gloves to protect your hands (IANNOTTI, 2021).

- ***Loosen the roots***

Once the plants are outside of the pot, gently pry apart the roots and shake off any clumps of soil. When you do this, the roots will have a much easier time acclimating to the new soil (IANNOTTI, 2021).

- ***Grip the plant and slip it out of the pot***

If you are unable to remove the plant from the pot, tilt the pot downwards and pull at the base of the plant. If your roses are bare roots, you need to unpackage the roots and then inspect them. Make sure to clip off any broken roots and roots that are infected with rot or wilting. After clipping the wilting parts off, soak the roots in water for about 12 hours before planting so that you can ensure that your plant doesn't dry out once it is planted (IANNOTTI, 2021).

Step #3: Plant the Rose

- ***Make a mound in the center of the hole***

For bare-root roses, make a mound of soil in the middle of the hole. Use a mixture of bone meal and remove soil so that the planted rose can have some nutrients. Pile the soil high enough so that when you place the rose bush on top of the mound, the knobby graft that is on the stem is barely below the soil level (IANNOTTI, 2021).

If you are transplanting a larger rose bush, prune them down so that they are about 6 to 8 inches long. When you plant it this way, the roots will be able to grow much easier without you having to add excessive amendments (IANNOTTI, 2021).

- ***Place the root ball in the hole***

If you are planting container roses, place the root ball in the hole. For bare-root roses, spread the roots so that they are down the sides. Fill the hole with soil and superphosphate and make sure that the roots are spread as far apart as possible. Separate the root ball in the planting hole and fill it with soil (IANNOTTI, 2021).

- ***The graft union should be fully buried***

When you plant the root ball, the graft union should be below the soil line. Once the plant is settled, the graft union should be fully buried into the ground and should be at least 1 to 2 inches deep. Continue filling the hole and gently pat it down so that the root zone is slightly compacted, and the plants stay intact (IANNOTTI, 2021).

Step #4: Give Water and Mulch

- ***Water deeply***

Water deeply after you are done planting. Water the new roses every other day, particularly if the weather is on the drier side. This is to ensure that your rose gets established; you will know that the rose has acclimated once it starts to produce new growth (IANNOTTI, 2021).

- ***1 to 2 inches of mulch***

It might also be a good idea to spread an inch or two of mulch over the new root zone of the rose plants, particularly around the base (IANNOTTI, 2021).

COMPANION PLANTING

What Is Companion Planting?

Companion planting basically refers to the act of growing different plants together, not only for convenience but also for mutual benefit. The majority of research done on companion planting actually focuses on vegetable or fruit gardens, but roses can also benefit from companion planting. In fact, you can prevent insect or disease infestations by companion planting. Companion planting is different from other gardening techniques because instead of focusing on scientific facts, you must use observation to find what works. You might have to go through a lot of trial and error to find out what works for you and your garden. But thinking of your garden as a system of biodiversity in which all plants are not only interconnected but also interdependent on one another helps you make a lot of better choices (Hassani, 2021).

Why Is Companion Planting Important?

There can be a lot of benefits of companion planting. Plants can attract beneficial insects and pollinators like bees, which are often essential for producing fruit or blooms. Companion plants can also act as insect repellents which means that you won't have to overuse pesticides or use pesticides at all. Some plants are even strong enough to fend off predators and undesirable wildlife. For example, raccoons dislike the smell of cucumbers, so if you use them as companion plants, not only will you be getting the cucumber itself, but you will also deter the raccoons from messing with your flowerbeds (Hassani, 2021).

Plants are also essential for improving soil fertility, and they do this by improving the supply of nutrients, uptake from the soil, and availability. Taller plants can act as a shade for smaller crops like lettuce, which often doesn't do well in the hot summer sun. Taller plants can also act as support for plants that need trellising. Interplanting can also help separate garden rows and distinguish faster-germinating plants from slower germinating ones. If companion planting is done well, you can even reduce the number of weeds (Hassani, 2021).

While companion planting benefits almost all plants, some plant pairs don't work together and stunt each other's growth. Generally, plants that compete with each other because they require similar types of nutrients, water, space, and sunlight aren't good pairs and shouldn't be planted next to each other because they will constantly compete. Crops that are susceptible to plant diseases like blight should be isolated from others because if the vulnerable plants catch the disease, it will quickly spread to the rest of the crops. Some plants also are poor companions; particularly, fennel is very competitive and is a poor companion plant. If you are planning to grow it, give it a separate and designated spot in the garden (Hassani, 2021).

Companion Plants with Roses

Plants do well with other plants that bring out their best qualities and share their space, without overpowering or paling in comparison. There are several things to take into consideration when picking out the best companion plant for your roses, and aesthetics is one of the most important. While you might not consider aesthetics as important, if you are looking to create a visually pleasing garden, you need to consider how plants will look next to each other (Iannotti, 2020).

Aesthetics

A. Things to Consider

Texture

The texture is important because you want to create a visually appealing background. This means you will need to pair bushy plants with skinner ones to break up the texture (Iannotti, 2020).

Color

Color is just as important as other aspects of your garden because you need to make sure that the flowers you are selecting not only complement each other but are also surrounded by plenty of green to bring out the most in them (Iannotti, 2020).

Form

The form of the plants can also play a vital part. If all your plants need a trellis to support them, then it won't be visually pleasing. Try to find plants that have different forms so that you can break up the monotony and introduce variety, just as you would with color (Iannotti, 2020).

B. Aesthetic Tips

Tall Complements Wide

Plants with tall spires complement wider and cup-shaped flowers like roses, whereas perennials and shrubs with green, silver, or purple leaves accentuate the rose blossoms. So, make sure to keep these things in mind while trying to choose a companion rose. Of course, you can forgo these tips if you want to create schemed gardens (Iannotti, 2020).

Provide Color Between the Main Roses

If you wish to extend the blooming period of your garden, then you can plant a few flowers that bloom between seasons or offset the colors of your roses. A good example of this is feathery purple and blue-gray catmint plants, offsetting pale pink roses and camouflaging blemishes in the rose foliage (Iannotti, 2020).

Growth

A. Lavender

Lavender and roses are considered to be classic pairs, and they are often planted very close to each other. The short purple blooms of the lavender offset the taller stems and cupped flowers of the roses beautifully. Not only that, but they often thrive in the same condition. Some varieties of roses love well-draining, which is also preferred by lavender plants. Lavender is also said to repel deer and rabbits and to attract the best pollinators in the world, bees. They are also very easy to care for and require little to no effort to maintain; so long as they get full sunlight, they can thrive without any setbacks (Moulton, 2021).

B. Catmint

Catmint is an aromatic herb that produces purplish-blue flowers that are almost identical to lavender. It is not only incredibly easy to grow, but it also is a natural insect repellent (Tilley, 2021).

C. Pinks

Pinks, also referred to as Dianthus, belong to the same family as carnations and emit a spicy fragrance. They come in a variety of stunning pink shades, which is why they are great for gardens that don't have a lot of color variety (Grant, 2022).

D. Heliotropes

This plant can be found in a variety of stunning colors like blue, lavender, and white and can beautifully offset any rose plants in your garden. The flowers are fragrant and said to attract hummingbirds and beneficial bacteria while repelling deer (Nardoozi, n.d.).

E. Lantana

Lantana is a unique vine-like plant with woody branches and is often found in outdoor hanging baskets. It has small, rounded clusters of flowers that may be yellow, blue, purple, pink, red, white, and even orange. The color of the flowers is so vibrant that they almost look fluorescent at times. They are incredibly fragrant and attract a variety of butterflies, particularly the spicebush swallowtail (Beauliew, 2022).

F. Verbena

If you are looking for plants that produce long-lasting blooms, then verbena is the plant to choose. They aren't particular about soil and can thrive as long as it is well-draining (Badgett, Verbena Plant Care: How to Grow Verbena Plants, 2021).

G. Petunia

Petunias can brighten dreary gardens with their lovely pastel-colored flowers. The best part about petunias is that they are incredibly easy to care for, so long as you water them weekly. Petunias are great pest controls and can repel beetles, leafhoppers, aphids, and tomato worms (Badgett, 2020).

Pest Protection

Good plants support each other while balancing each other's flaws. Some companion plants are amazing at repelling or discouraging pests, and they do that without you having to use chemicals. Chemicals can often kill pollinators and harm the flowers. Some members of the onion family, particularly chives, increase the scent of roses while warding off aphids and preventing black spots. Herbs and other plants that make wonderful rose companions and repel pests are scented geraniums, parsley, thyme, marigolds, sage, rue, catmint, feverfew, anise-hyssop, yarrow, oregano, and lavender. Tomatoes are also said to prevent black spots, but most gardeners avoid pairing the two (Iannotti, 2020).

In this chapter, we discussed the best time and the best way to plant roses. We also talked about companion planting and why it is important. In the next chapter, we will focus on the fourth set of the F.L.O.W.E.R.S. method: caring for the roses.

CHAPTER 5

WHAT'S AND HOW'S OF ROSE CARE

"Do not watch the petals fall from the rose with sadness, know that, like life, things sometimes must fade, before they can bloom again."

— ANONYMOUS

In the last few chapters, we have been focusing on how to choose roses and plant them. Now that your roses are planted, let us focus our attention on taking care of the roses. Before we move on to the tips that can help us ensure that our plants remain healthy and produce great flowers throughout the seasons, let's talk about the health benefits of roses.

Roses have always been popular and are known around the world as a symbol of everlasting love and devotion, but did you know that roses have a lot of health benefits? Roses are rich in antioxidants, which is why it is considered a medicinal flower. Tea that is made from rose petals tends to strengthen the digestive system, and it is also great for boosting the immune system while preventing different diseases. Rose tea is also considered to be a much better way to lose weight while staying hydrated. Some other benefits of roses include expelling toxins from the body, eliminating body fat, and preventing urinary tract infections. Rose extracts are also used in skin and hair care. All of this proves that roses don't just enhance the beauty of your garden, but they also have a lot of medicinal benefits that could make growing them worthwhile (Menon, 2022).

WATERING

How Often Should You Water a Rose Bush?

Just like roses love sunlight, they also love water. An accurate amount of water helps the roses grow and promotes the formation of large and long-lasting flowers that have a rich color and thick, sturdy petals. This is because water-primarily functions as transport and takes the nutrients through the roots and the leaves. If the plant receives too little water, it wilts. On the other hand, if you overwater, the roots are unable to get any oxygen, and the leaves turn yellow and fall off (Properly Water Roses, n.d.).

The Key to Watering Roses

- Determining the time

Soil, surrounding plants, and the temperature affect how much water your plants need and how frequently you need to water them. In warmer climates, weekly waterings are enough, and two inches of water per week, 4 to 5 gallons, may be all that is needed to help the plant thrive. However, if the soil is sandy and the weather is hot, windy, or dry, you may need to water the garden more frequently (Properly Water Roses, n.d.).

- Journaling the last water

It is also a good idea to journal all the watering because it will help you keep track of the frequency of watering and avoid over or underwatering the plants. The best way to care for your plants is to water deeply so that your plants can establish a deeper root system. Light watering will result in shallow roots, leaving the plants more susceptible to summer heat and frost. So, consider watering deeply and slowly (Properly Water Roses, n.d.).

- How often do you need to water?

Test the soil with your finger to find out when you need to water the roses. If the soil is completely dry, your plants need to be watered. If it is muddy, there might be too much water but not enough drainage. Another way of figuring out if your plants are getting too much water is by checking the leaves, because overwatered plants have yellow leaves. However, if your leaves are dry and crispy, there is insufficient water for your roses. On the other hand, moist soil indicates that your plants have the right amount of water (Properly Water Roses, n.d.).

How to Water Rose Bushes?

General Watering Tips

- 1 to 2 inches of water each week

You should give your plants 1 to 2 inches of water in a single session every week from early spring until fall. Once the weather turns hot, dry, and humid, increase the frequency of the watering to every three to four days. If your soil is porous, it will benefit from additional deep soakings (Neveln, 2015).

- Soak the soil to a 16-to-18-inch depth

If you lightly water your plants, it might do more damage than good because the roots won't grow deep enough and will be more vulnerable to frost and heat. Plants with weaker roots are also easily injured by cultivation and prone to burns caused by fertilizers (Neveln, 2015).

- Water roses early in the day

Water roses super early in the day and do it at ground level. This can help prevent the spread of diseases like black spot (Properly Water Roses, n.d.).

- Avoid wetting the foliage

Avoid wetting the foliage routinely, especially when overcast. This is because watering the foliage can encourage the spread of disease. Instead, spray your rose bush with water if it is absolutely necessary and only do it on a sunny day. A spray nozzle has enough force to clear the leaves of any dust, dirt, spider mites, and other insects (Properly Water Roses, n.d.).

- Use mulch to conserve water

If you wish to conserve water and improve the water retention rate, then you need to try mulching. You can conserve up to 50 percent of water by mulching. In addition, a 2-to-3-inch layer of mulch can suppress the weeds and cool down the soil, lowering the temperature 10 to 20 degrees. You could either get your hands on mulch from a local nursery or create your own by shredding a newspaper. Aged sawdust, manure, grass clippings, hay, and compost are also great mulching choices (Properly Water Roses, n.d.).

MORE WATERING TIPS

TIP #1: Be diligent

Diligently water your roses if you want them to produce big and healthy blooms (Boeckmann, 2019).

TIP #2: Soak the entire root

When watering roses, ensure you thoroughly soak the ground until the entire root is wet. This will help your plants establish healthy, strong, and deep roots (Boeckmann, 2019).

TIP #3: Avoid shallow sprinklings

Avoid shallow sprinkling since they can do more harm than

good. Shallow sprinkling won't reach deeper roots, which may encourage the growth of fungus (Boeckmann, 2019).

Tip #4: Do not allow roses to completely dry out

During the fall, reduce the amount of water but avoid letting the plants completely dry out (Boeckmann, 2019).

Tip #5: They can drown if you aren't careful

Roses love water, but they can drown if you aren't careful. They don't like sitting in water and will actually die if the soil is too wet, especially in the winter. The ideal soil should be rich and loose, with good drainage. One of the worst things you can do to your roses is rob them of adequate drainage (Boeckmann, 2019).

PROPAGATING

- What is propagating?

Propagation simply means to reproduce a plant easily from a simple cutting of the plant. Unlike seeds, which have the ability to produce different types of plants, propagated plants are a replica of their parent plants; you don't have to be trained at propagating roses to be able to do this because roses are fairly easy to propagate (Hansen, n.d.).

- What can propagating do for roses?

Propagating has a lot of benefits, but the most prominent one is that you can essentially continue to multiply your prized roses at a fraction of the cost. Along with personal use, propagation can be essential to restoring native plant species or prized and rare rose species. Propagating is also beneficial in creating hybrids between different rose species and cloning their desirable characteristics. People have been breeding plants for a long time, trying to develop plants that only have desirable characteristics like hardiness, superior blooms, amazing smell, and those that are visually pleasing (Plant Propagation Techniques and Benefits, 2021).

- What are rose cuttings?

ROSE CUTTINGS basically refer to pieces of rose stem that are taken from a rose plant during different stages of maturity. Some plants are very particular about the types of cutting that you need to take for them to root, but roses are pretty flexible. The rose cuttings only need to be taken from new stems that have sprouted this year and are at three main growth stages: softwood, semi-hardwood, and hardwood (Hansen, n.d.).

- Softwood cuttings are the easiest and the fastest to root. They can be taken in early summer and late spring. During this time, the flexible new stems have just started to mature. Prime softwood cuttings are taken from pencil-sized stems (Hansen, n.d.).
- Semi-hardwood cuttings are taken in late summer and early fall. During this time, the rose stems have matured a little, and they have firm rosehips forming on the plant (Hansen, n.d.).
- Hardwood cuttings are the hardest to propagate because they take root very slowly. They are taken in late fall or early winter when the new stems of the year have matured, entered dormancy, and hardened (Hansen, n.d.).

When is the best time to propagate?

THE BEST TIME TO take a propagating cutting from plants is when they grow vigorously, typically during early summer. The stems should neither be brand new nor fully mature and, if possible, choose stems that have fading flowers which are flowers that have shed their petals. A stem that has a budding flower is too young for propagating. After you cut off the stem, you should immediately dip the end in growth hormone and plant it directly inside the soil (Propagating Roses, n.d.).

How to Propagate Roses

Step #1: Choose the right cutting

Choose a cutting that is healthy because it will obviously

increase the chances of the propagation sprouting (Propagating Roses, n.d.).

Step #2: Go for the upper part of the plant

Take the cutting either from the upper part of the plant or from the side of the plant. This is because the cuttings that are taken from the middle part of the plants don't end up rooting well (Propagating Roses, n.d.).

Step #3: Select a stem that is 4 to 5 inches long

If you plan to propagate them, make sure that the stem you select is at least 4 to 5 inches long and has at least 2 to 3 leaves attached. Leaves produce sugars and hormones by the process of photosynthesis which helps facilitate the rooting process (Propagating Roses, n.d.).

Step #4: Use the right blade or pruning shears

Use a sharp razor blade or sharp pruning shears to cut the stems for propagation. Make a clean slice at a 45-degree angle to maximize the rooting area. Cuttings root best if the slice is made directly underneath the leaf node (Propagating Roses, n.d.).

Step #5: Remove the flowers or buds from the cutting

Remove any flowers or buds from the rose cutting; also make sure to remove any lower leaves. Cut the remaining leaves in half to reduce the loss of moisture through the process of transpiration. Less foliage will maximize the amount of energy the cutting will expend on developing the roots instead of maintaining the leaves (Propagating Roses, n.d.).

Step #6: Dip the bottom two inches of the cutting into the cloning solution

Dip the bottom two inches of the cutting in cloning solution or rooting hormone immediately after cutting the stem. Rooting hormone is not always necessary, but it will improve the chances of the propagation rooting (Propagating Roses, n.d.).

Step #7: Make a hole in the growing medium

Use a pencil to make a small hole in the soil or any other growing medium you have selected. The hole should be big enough to fit the stem comfortably. Then, gently tap the area surrounding the cutting to secure it in place (Propagating Roses, n.d.).

Step #8: Cover with a jar

Cover the propagating stem with a jar or put the whole container into a plastic bag to create a greenhouse effect, which will help maintain high levels of humidity (Propagating Roses, n.d.).

Step #9: Keep it moist until roots appear

Roses root best in bright light, so set your plants in the window and always provide warmth from the bottom using a heating mat. However, make sure you avoid overheating the plant. Keep the growing media moist and wait until the roots appear. The roots can appear in only 3 to 4 weeks. Slowly "harden" the plant before transplanting it into the growing pot (Propagating Roses, n.d.).

AFTERCARE

After you have planted your roses, you need to continue to take care of them in order to get large, healthy, and beautiful roses. Here are a few things you should watch out for:

Fertilizing

What nutrients do roses need?

There are three primary nutrients that roses need in order to thrive. These include Nitrogen, Phosphorus, and Potassium.

Nitrogen

Nitrogen encourages healthy and rapid leaf reproduction, and because the rose depends on its foliage to grow the flowers, rich foliage naturally translates to more abundant and beautiful flowers. Too much nitrogen can promote and boost foliage production, but it will cut down the bloom production, while less nitrogen will result in yellow leaves, a stunted plant, and small and poorly developed roses. So, there are drawbacks of both under and over-feeding, which is why we need to be especially careful about feeding nitrogen to plants (Loughrey, n.d.).

Phosphorus

Phosphorus is primarily responsible for root development and the production of flowers. The absence of phosphorus causes leaf drops, weak flower stems, and even buds that refuse to open and bloom (Loughrey, n.d.).

Potassium

Potassium is incredibly beneficial for plants, especially those a little more vulnerable to diseases, because it helps roses recover when they are damaged by diseases, extreme weather conditions, or insects. Conversely, the lack of potassium can result in yellow margins on the leaf, poor development of the buds, and weak flower stems (Loughrey, n.d.).

How to fertilize

- *Rich organic matter*

If you are planning on amending the soil, use rich organic matter to do so. Start fertilizing when the leaves appear, and the chances of severe spring frosts have blown over. The fertilization schedule should be based on how long and how often your roses bloom. The general rule of thumb is to fertilize every bloom cycle, but you can gradually reduce the amount of fertilizer each time. Stop fertilizing 6 to 8 weeks before the first frost because you don't want your plants to grow during the winter seasons. You can start fertilizing the roses again after they go dormant. Adding fertilizer at that point won't harm the plants and will instead prepare them for spring (Hassani, 2022).

Container roses, however, may need to be fertilized more often than plants growing in soil. Fertilize them every growing season or when the foliage starts looking chlorotic, indicating nutrient deficiency (Hassani, 2022).

- *Slow-release fertilizer*

You can also try working slow-release fertilizer into the soil, along with a handful of bone meal. This mixture will promote healthy root development. Make sure to read the instructions on the box before applying this to the soil (Loughrey, n.d.).

- *Sprinkling 1/4th to ½ cup of Epsom salt*

If you are looking to promote cane and foliage growth, sprinkle ¼ or ½ cup of Epsom salt around the base of the rose bushes or plants (Loughrey, n.d.).

The best fertilizers

- *Organic*

Organic fertilizers are often derived from natural elements or matter that hail from animals and plants, making them incredibly eco-friendly. Different types of organic fertilizers have various nutritional benefits, and they can be used both alone and combined with other items in your rose-feeding regimen. Some types of organic fertilizers can even help you improve soil texture and support the formation of beneficial microbes (Loughrey, n.d.).

- *Inorganic*

Inorganic fertilizers are synthetic, man-made, or chemical and are always found in the market, ready for use. This is why they are incredibly convenient, less expensive, and more concentrated than their organic counterparts. However, these products do nothing to improve soil quality and don't have a lot of residual benefits. In fact, some inorganic fertilizers could contain insecticides, which should be avoided altogether because they can harm wildlife (Loughrey, n.d.).

- *Compost*

Compost is great for improving overall plant health and helps the plants become more resilient to diseases and different kinds of pests. Mix the compost into the soil during the planting time and apply a layer 1 to 2 inches thick around the base of established rose plants during the growing season (Loughrey, n.d.).

- *Manure*

Manure can be used during planting time and on already established rose plants. Just make sure that the manure you acquire is well-aged, so it doesn't burn the plants. If you are looking for something lighter, try applying manure tea (Loughrey, n.d.).

- *Bone meal*

Bone meal can be added to the soil during spring to get a slow-release effect throughout the entire growing season. You can also apply it during fall to promote root growth and flower production (Loughrey, n.d.).

- *Cottonseed meal*

This helps boost overall plant health. You need to only apply it once or twice a year for the slow-release effect that will last you all growing season. Since cottonseed meal is acidic in nature, the soil pH might need to be adjusted by using lime or other kinds of alkaline matter (Loughrey, n.d.).

- *Kelp meal*

Kelp meal facilitates root development and boosts immunity so that plants can defend against diseases and pests. Because of this fact, it can become a regular part of your growing program (Loughrey, n.d.).

- *Fish fertilizer*

Fish fertilizer can be used as an all-purpose fertilizer since it helps promote the lush growth of plants. If you are planning on making fish fertilizer your primary one, you need to apply it every 3 weeks during the entire growing season. Fish fertilizer is also often used in combination with kelp (Loughrey, n.d.).

- *Alfalfa*

This might be one of the best organic amendments available on the market, especially for roses. This is because it promotes vigorous growth and increases the production of the blooms dramatically (Loughrey, n.d.).

- *Coffee grounds*

If you have coffee grounds on hand, you can sprinkle some around the base of the rose bushes anytime during the growing season. This will give the plant a boost of nitrogen it needs to continue growing vigorously. However, coffee is acidic in nature, so you might need to make some amendments to the soil with lime to maintain the ideal soil pH (Loughrey, n.d.).

- *Epsom salts*

Epsom salts are great for improving the color of the blooms and the color of the foliage. They are also great at promoting cane growth. Apply Epsom salt when you are planting a rose plant or anytime during the spring season (Loughrey, n.d.).

Mulching

Mulching your roses can help you save a lot of water, reduce the temperature of the soil, and prevent evaporation of water. It also helps you suppress weed growth which often competes with roses for moisture. Mulches are also great for evening out rapid changes in soil moisture which can cause a lot of problems during hot and humid weather (Beckstrom, 2016).

Composite manure makes for a really good mulch since it provides the soil with necessary nutrients while still looking decent. Make sure that the manure you have selected is fully composted and avoid adding too much. Horse manure is the safest option so mix it in a 50/50 ratio with other organic compost. If you do this, you won't risk damaging your roses, but you will still get the nitrogen (Beckstrom, 2016).

How to mulch your roses

- *Feed your roses*

Before you even think about mulching, feed your roses and the surrounding soil. You should also clear the ground, so it is free of any weeds and old leaves (How to Mulch Your Roses, n.d.).

- *Water the soil*

Give your plants and soil a bunch of water, so the ground is completely saturated before you add a layer of mulch on top. Use old and well-rotted manure; if possible, source it from a local farm. The manure should be at least 2 years old. This is because fresh manure can actually burn your plants and roses (How to Mulch Your Roses, n.d.).

- *Apply a 2.5 to 5 cm layer of mulch*

Apply a 2.5 to 5 cm layer of mulch around the base of your roses and spread the mulch out, so it at least encompasses the width of your rose canopy. Your mulching layer must be super thick if you want to mulch effectively. It is always a good idea to mulch before the weeds start growing (How to Mulch Your Roses, n.d.).

When to mulch

- *Late March*

Start mulching in later March so that your ground can be protected from the heat of summer (How to Mulch Your Roses, n.d.).

- *Early April*

You could also start mulching in early April (How to Mulch Your Roses, n.d.).

- *After the first feed*

You could also start mulching after the first feed. And if the layer of mulch has disappeared by autumn, you can consider adding a second layer because it will be incredibly beneficial before winter (How to Mulch Your Roses, n.d.).

CHAPTER 6

ENTER THE LIFE OF PRUNING

“The purpose of pruning is to improve the quality of the roses, not to hurt the bush.”

— FLORENCE LITTAUER

Even though pruning is necessary for the long-term health of roses, it is quite hard to figure out how exactly you need to prune them. This is because there are so many different types of rose plants. But you don't need to worry! In this chapter, you will be given the information you need to be able to proceed with the process of pruning. Aside from that, you will also be guided through the pruning steps and will learn some tips and tricks for pruning plants, particularly roses.

Pruning is basically the reduction of the overall tree size, which is caused by the removal of excess tree tissue. Pruning has a lot of benefits and potential for regulating tree vigor. The growth that follows after pruning is affected both directly and indirectly by the pruning itself. Therefore, you need to consider the effects of pruning on tree growth and size before you can proceed. In addition to growth and size, you also need to consider the age of the tree, growth, and fruiting/flowering habits, the stage of development the plant is going through, and finally, the environment the tree is exposed to (Stiles, 1984).

PRUNING

What Is Pruning?

Nature has always been untamable, which is why trees grow freely and spread their limbs out and up towards the sky. The older branches naturally fall to the ground, and newer ones replace them. However, trees that grow with human intervention don't really have as much freedom because humans want to get the most out of their plants; roses are no exception, and we use pruning to achieve that. Pruning is basically when you selectively remove dead, old, or dying branches from a tree. The goal is to remove unwanted or odd branches from the tree to improve its structure and promote new and healthy growth (WHAT IS PRUNING? THE IMPORTANCE, BENEFITS AND METHODS OF PRUNING, 2018).

What Is the Importance of Pruning Roses?

Pruning is one of the best things you can do for your plants because a proper prune is an investment since it helps maintain your plants for a long time. It also helps improve the overall look and ensures that you and your loved ones are safe from any falling branches. When you trim a tree, you remove dead, damaged, and broken branches. In addition to that, you also encourage your plants to produce new growth. It is also possible to train trees by pruning them. Trained trees don't interrupt power lines and neither do they hang over roofs. Lastly, pruning trees helps the plant create a solid foundation which encourages long-term health (WHAT IS PRUNING? THE IMPORTANCE, BENEFITS AND METHODS OF PRUNING, 2018).

Benefits of Pruning

Pruning can be an excellent preventive maintenance method for both young and established plants. A regular pruning schedule can benefit both the tree and the gardener for the long-term. Here are a few benefits of investing your time and money in pruning trees.

Benefit #1: Promote plant health

Pruning can help you get rid of dead or decaying branches and stubs, and by doing so, you can allow your plant to produce new growth. This not only makes your plants healthier but also protects your property and other pedestrians from damage. Pruning can also deter infestations of different kinds. The best part is that when you prune away dead or infested branches, it prevents insects and other kinds of growth from making a home on your plant and ultimately harming them. So, pruning your trees can help save the life of your tree and prevent financial loss (The Importance of Pruning: Protect Your Plants and Property, n.d.).

Benefit #2: Maintain your plants

Pruning also helps you maintain your shrubs and trees, and it encourages healthy flower and fruit production. Regular trimming can also help you develop aesthetic hedges and keep plants proportioned and dense. This kind of maintenance adds support to your property's appearance (The Importance of Pruning: Protect Your Plants and Property, n.d.).

Benefit #3: Protects your property

Regular pruning can help you reduce the risk of structural or storm damage by removing broken branches preemptively. In addition, it will protect your friends and family from broken and falling branches. As previously stated, it will also help control vermin, pests, and even snakes by removing their habitat options (The Importance of Pruning: Protect Your Plants and Property, n.d.).

Benefit #4: Stimulate or suppress growth

If you prune your trees a certain way, you can promote new growth while suppressing unwanted growth. Get rid of any overgrowth, even if you must prune it a little more aggressively. You can promote new growth by picking specific branches and pruning them more sparsely (4 Benefits of Pruning Your Trees, n.d.).

Benefit #5: Makes your plant feel safer

Pruning can keep lower branches from becoming too large and potentially dangerous. For example, you can prune smaller trees and keep the foliage from blocking the sidewalk or prevent it from rubbing against and damaging other foliage (4 Benefits of Pruning Your Trees, n.d.).

THE PRUNING PHASES

Reasons for Pruning Roses

Pruning to reduce the size

If you are pruning so that you can fit a bigger plant inside a smaller space, then you should know that it works well with some kinds of varieties, particularly hybrid tea and shrub roses. To do this kind of pruning, you need to cut each branch back until you reach an outward-facing bud. Roses can survive even if you cut off huge chunks of branches but ensure you don't remove more than ⅓ to ½ of the overall plant growth. Hybrid tea roses should have a vase-like shape after the pruning is completed. On the other hand, shrub roses should be uniform but should have an overall reduced size (How to Prune Roses, n.d.).

Pruning to remove dead and diseased growth

Pruning diseased and damaged growth on your plants is essential because insects can take up residence on the dead branches, making them their home and ultimately multiplying on them. In addition, you can easily spot dead branches because they have a completely different color than branches that are alive and well. Remove all the old, diseased, and dead wood from the branches and the entire plant so that the only thing left is healthy and green (How to Prune Roses, n.d.).

Pruning to promote airflow

Roses can often get moldy or start hosting other harmful bacteria if they don't get enough air and ventilation. However, you can prune your plants and improve airflow at the same time. All you need to do is remove branches that are crossing each other and growing at the center of the shrub. Always cut the plant back to an outward-facing bud. You can remove up to one-half of the growth from inside the center of the shrub to promote air movement (How to Prune Roses, n.d.).

Pruning to rejuvenate growth

Some shrubs, particularly rose shrubs, benefit from renewal pruning. During this kind of pruning, you remove one-third of the plant's growth each year, starting with the oldest growth of that year. Cut back the oldest branches until you reach the ground and only leave about two-thirds of the branches behind. As the plant produces new growth, it will also bloom profusely. When spring arrives, remove another one-third of the old growth but do it evenly throughout the shrub (How to Prune Roses, n.d.).

What Do You Need to Prune Roses?

You will need gardening gloves to protect your hands while you handle the thorny branches of the rose plants. Bypass pruning shears can help you easily cut off rose branches, and long-handled loppers can help you prune parts of the plants that you wouldn't normally be able to reach. It is also a good idea to keep white glue and other kinds of mediums on hand to protect the fresh cuts after you prune the roses (Iannotti, 2022).

When to prune your roses?

- Spring

Most of the pruning should be done during early spring and after the last frost for people living in colder climates. If you can't figure out the time properly, you can always let your plant tell you. You can typically start pruning when they start to bud or leaf out (Hagen, 2022).

- Summer

If you want to cut down some dead flowers, you can do that anytime during the summer. A long-time rose breeder, David Austin, said that if you deadhead and remove dead roses from the shrubs during the flowering season, your plant is more likely to produce more blooms, and you will also maintain an attractive-looking shrub (Hagen, 2022).

- Fall

After the first frost passes, trim bigger and longer stems so that they don't snap during the storms that are common during winters. Doing this can prevent your roses from getting too top-heavy and accidentally uprooting in the strong winds. Any branches that are crossing and rubbing with each other should also be trimmed back to minimize potential damage. However, take it easy because pruning can often encourage new growth, which is something you want to avoid in the dead of winter. Make sure to remove any dead and diseased branches or foliage and clean your tools in between to prevent transferring diseases from one plant to another (Hagen, 2022).

Steps To Pruning

Step #1: Removing the remaining leaves

If you are pruning, you should first take a little bit of time to study the rose bush, noticing its overall shape and health, and then go into pruning. Start from the bottom of the plant, pruning off dead canes present at the bottom and then moving upwards, opening up the plant to allow air and light to flow in. If you are unable to see the shape of the rose bush and plant, trim off all the leaves so that you can see all the stems. This will also remove any diseases and pests that might be fostered in the foliage during winter (Hagen, 2022) (Iannotti, 2022).

Step #2: Start with dead wood

Find old-looking wood and trace it to the point where the green fades into brown. Cut the plant at that point, at a 45-degree angle, making sure to take special care of the white flesh inside. If the flesh that is revealed isn't white, cut down until it turns white since it indicates healthy flesh (Iannotti, 2022).

Step #3: Open up the center

Take off any crossing branches since they can run against each other, damaging themselves, and eventually encouraging the spread of disease. The end goal is to have branches that reach the sky and have an open structure that almost resembles a vase. Remove any canes that are thinner than pencils since these branches take up a lot of nutrients and produce little to no blooms (Hagen, 2022) (Iannotti, 2022).

Step #4: Remove the weak growth

Remove weak-looking growth as well as any suckers. Suckers are basically branches that grow vertically towards the sky instead of out or parallel to other branches. These branches don't produce any flowers, and even if by some miracle blooms do blossom on them, the flowers are far inferior to those produced on regular branches (Hagen, 2022) (Iannotti, 2022).

Step #5: Prune the canes

Prune the canes by cutting 1/4" or 1/2" above the bud eye, a small bump that is found where a leaf would typically emerge from the plant. The newer stems grow towards the direction of the bud, and the goal is to encourage them to grow outwards. Make the cut on the cane at a 45-degree angle, sloping away from the bud itself and allowing any excess water to run off the plant (Hagen, 2022).

Step #6 Seal any fresh cuts

If you think your freshly cut canes could be vulnerable to rot and rose borers, then seal the cut with a pruning sealer. But, if you can't get your hands on it, use white glue (Hagen, 2022).

Step #7: Clean up the bush

After you are done with the pruning, clean up the surrounding area so that it is free of any fallen leaves and branches. This is because the leaves could cultivate and continue to harbor pests and other diseases (Hagen, 2022).

Step #8: Feed them

After pruning, your roses will need a lot of nutrients to rebuild their branches and produce new blooms; after all, roses are big eaters. Therefore, you need to feed them with a good fertilizer (Hagen, 2022).

This chapter focused on pruning, particularly when you need to prune, how to do it, and what you need to prune your roses. In the next chapter, we will focus on the next step of the F.L.O.W.E.R.S. method - the remedies.

CHAPTER 7
REMEDY THE DISEASES AND PESTS

"As delicate as flower, as tender as rose petals, choosing to be tender and kind in a harsh environment is not weakness, it's courage."

— LUFFINA LOURDURAJ

Roses have always been revered for their beauty, fragrance, and even their healing properties. Roses are considered a symbol of achievement or completion because, after a long, thorny stem, you are awarded a flower that is beautiful and mesmerizing. For some, roses are even a metaphor for life because they show that after overcoming difficulty, you will find happiness, harmony, and union. Roses are symbolic, and aside from being used to express love or war, they also symbolize silence and secrecy, and this symbol goes back to the ancient Egyptians and Greeks. People who were involved with mysteries and existed pre-Christianity wore roses during ceremonies to indicate that they would keep any and all secrets that were passed down to them. In fact, in many countries, it was customary to hang roses over secret meetings and gatherings, which sprung a new word into the world called "sub-rose," which means under the rose or in simpler words, confidential (Charlow, 2012).

The colors of the roses also have symbolic meanings. Each rose, even the shape and age of the blossom, conveys a very different meaning or gives a silent message. The traditional red roses symbolize romance, courage, love, and beauty. They also signify purity, and a thornless red rose means love at first sight. A yellow rose symbolizes friendship, joy, and new beginnings. Orange roses symbolize sensuality, fascination, and desire. Pink roses, particularly dark pink roses, indicate gratitude and appreciation. On the other hand, baby pink roses symbolize sympathy and admiration. Lastly, white roses symbolize innocence or purity, and at the same time, they symbolize secrecy, silence, and reverence (Charlow, 2012).

When you grow roses, you will naturally interact with a lot of pests and diseases. This chapter will focus on the common pests and diseases that attack roses, as well as how to deal with or treat them.

DISEASES AND TREATMENT

Roses are prolific all around the world, and there are many different types, but plant varieties have different resistance to pests and diseases. Even if you carefully select a variety of roses to try and avoid diseases and pests, your roses might still be susceptible to them. Therefore, you need to learn how to spot different diseases and how to treat them (ROSE DISEASES, 2021).

Blackspot

- **What is blackspot for roses?**

Blackspot is a serious but very common rose disease that can easily become an epidemic during the growing season. A type of fungus called the Diplocarpon rosae causes blackspot on the roses. The disease hits hardest after particularly long, wet, and warm periods. The symptoms can occur as circular black spots on the leaves, which can grow to be ½ inches in diameter, and these spots are also surrounded by a yellow area. The infection continues throughout the summer months. The immature woods can develop raised purplish-red irregular blotches. The disease can stunt plant growth and cause it to produce fewer and paler flowers. The disease spreads so fast that by midsummer, your roses might lose all their leaves (ROSE DISEASES, 2021).

Even though the advanced symptom of this disease features

black spots much like the name, you can actually spot this disease pretty early on if you are vigilant. The initial symptoms start with feathery-edged, black spots on the lower leaves, and as the disease spreads, the leaves turn fully yellow and fall off (Black Spot Disease of Roses, 2021).

- **How to treat it?**

Resistant varieties

If you want to make sure that your plants are particularly resistant to black spots, you can plant blackspot-resistant varieties such as Pride N Joy which is a hybrid tea rose, Sexy Rexy, which is a floribunda, and Prima Donna, which is a Grandiflora.

MAINTAIN good sanitation

Maintaining good sanitation is critical in reducing the development of the disease in the future. During fall or winter, remove all the older leaves from the ground, as well as all the mulch that contains the infected leaves. Replace everything with a fresh layer of mulch before the new growth begins during the spring (ROSE DISEASES, 2021).

REMOVE and destroy infected canes

As we previously discussed, canes that have blackspot have dark or reddish-purple lesions. To save the plant, you need to cut back the infected canes and dispose of them. Severely infected plants need to be pruned back within 1 to 2 inches of the bud union during winter or early spring. Remove and dispose of the infected leaves as they appear during the growing season (ROSE DISEASES, 2021).

Dry leaves

It is best not to have overhead irrigation methods for your roses, especially during the late afternoon or early evening. Soaker hoses are an excellent way to water your roses and conserve water. You can also promote rapid drying of leaves by planting the roses in full sunlight. Another thing you can do is space the plants apart so that they have good circulation (ROSE DISEASES, 2021).

Powdery Mildew

- **What is powdery mildew?**

Powdery mildew is another disease that is both serious and widespread. It is a type of fungus called the Sphaerotheca Pannosa Var. Rosae, and it causes a grayish-white powdery substance to grow on the surface of the leaves, shoots, and even the buds. The disease causes the infected leaves to distort and can even cause leaf drops. In addition to that, the roses may also produce poor quality roses, and some may fail to open. Initially, mildew starts as white growth, but as it ages, it could turn to brown, which could make it harder to diagnose and treat. The disease may occur anytime during the growing season when the temperature is especially mild, particularly between 70-to-80-degrees Fahrenheit, and the humidity is high during the night and low during the day. The disease is most severe in shady areas and during colder periods (ROSE DISEASES, 2021).

- **How to treat it?**

Resistant varieties

Rose varieties differ in their susceptibility to powdery mildew, and resistant varieties naturally fair better against the disease. Some resistant varieties include Duet, Eiffel Tower, Grand Slam, Jamaica, Matterhorn, Golden Slipper, Saratoga, Camelot, John S. Armstrong, Pink Parfait, Queen Elizabeth, Carefree Wonder, and All That Jazz (ROSE DISEASES, 2021).

Remove and destroy diseased leaves

Remove and destroy all diseased leaves and canes during the growing season. Rake up all the fallen leaves and destroy them as well. If the disease is very severe, you can select a chemical to control the spread of the fungus. If you are going to choose a fungicide, choose one that can control both powdery mildew and blackspot. Some fungicides that can be used in home gardens include propiconazole, sulfur, neem oil, baking soda mixed with horticultural oil, thiophanate methyl, and myclobutanil. Apply all the chemicals according to the directions on the back of the box or label (ROSE DISEASES, 2021).

If you are looking for a non-chemical form of disease control, you can try planting your roses in full sunlight, shade-loving roses obviously being the exception. Climbers and ramblers grown with good circulation are less likely to be affected than plants that get stagnant air, and bush roses grown in sheltered areas are more likely to be affected. You could also manage the soil to try and control the spread of powdery mildew. Provide good soil drainage and water regularly during drier periods because plants suffering from regular droughts are more susceptible. Applying mulch may also help with the retention of water. You also need to feed the plants regularly to promote growth, however, avoid giving them too much nitrogen since that can encourage "soft" growth which is prone to fungus (Rose powdery mildew, n.d.).

Another thing you can do is avoid planting too densely and give space between the plants. Aim for an open environment to increase circulation. Pruning can also help increase circulation, so prune your roses to an open structure. Avoid watering the leaves and the stem during the morning and evening. However, overhead watering during dry weather can reduce powdery mildew since the fungus doesn't like direct contact with water. At the same time, avoid keeping the leaves wet for long periods of time since it can help fester other kinds of diseases like rust and blackspot (Rose powdery mildew, n.d.).

Stem Canker and Dieback

A. What is it?

Cankers usually appear as discolored or dead areas on rose canes and vary in color from light tan to dark purplish brown. This can be caused by various species of fungi, including Cryptosporella, Botryosphaeria, Coniothyrium, and Leptosphaeria. These fungi enter into the healthy canes through wounds caused by improper pruning, flower cutting, wind, winter injury, and hail damage. Cankers can continue to grow until they surround the cane or reach the crown of the plant, spreading to the other canes or killing the plant. They commonly happen to roses that have poor nutrition, winter injury, or are weakened by blackspot (ROSE DISEASES, 2021).

The fungi that cause stem canker and dieback usually survive the winter on diseased canes and plant debris. Spores of the causal fungi are usually spread by wind-blown rain or through irrigation. Rose canes are infected through wounds during periods of humid and wet weather. The disease can also be spread by fungus-contaminated pruning tools. Cankers often form on the stub of pruned canes and can also be found around the leaves or thorn scars (Drinkard, 2013).

B. How to treat it?

There is no fungicide that can help control stem canker. Keep the plants healthy by controlling blackspot, powdery mildew, and insects. Here are some things that can help minimize the spread of the disease (ROSE DISEASES, 2021).

Avoid damaging the plant

Avoid damaging the plant while cultivating, flower cutting, pruning, or transplanting. Wounds are a major way the fungus enters the plant.

Learn how to prune properly

Make sure to prune properly so that you don't create any wounds that can help the fungus enter. Always prune an outward-facing bud since this will help avoid too many branches growing into the center of the plant, which can cause the branches to cross and rub together, creating lesions.

Remove all infected parts of the canes

Make a pruning cut a little below the diseased area and prune about one-fourth inch above an outward-facing bud node, without cutting the nodal tissue, at a 45-degree angle. Prune live canes in the spring, not during the fall. Disinfect cutting tools after using them on diseased plants in a solution of one part household bleach and nine parts water (ROSE DISEASES, 2021).

Rust

A. What is it?

Rose rust is a fungal disease that is common in the western U.S. While it isn't a major rose pathogen, it can be bothersome to some rose gardeners because it diminishes the quality of the roses, and if it is left unchecked, it can completely defoliate and kill the plants. The disease itself is caused by a fungus in the genus Phragmidium, which causes orange-colored spots to appear on stems and leaves. When the rust gets severe, a cloud of orange dust may be found on the surface of the plant or on the ground below. Rose rust attacks almost all plant parts, with the exception of the roots and petals. Severely diseased leaves might turn yellow or brown and then drop (ROSE DISEASES, 2021) (Shires, n.d.).

B. How to treat rust?

Give good air circulation

Similar to other fungal diseases, the chances of your plants catching rust dramatically decrease if you provide them with good air circulation. If you have a greenhouse, try to avoid condensation and other sources of free-flowing water since that can promote humidity which means more chances of fungal diseases and bacteria (ROSE DISEASES, 2021) (Shires, n.d.).

Do not create crowded areas with the plants

A good rule of thumb while planting roses is to give them plenty of room to not only grow but also get the sunlight and air circulation they need to thrive (ROSE DISEASES, 2021).

Prune them to keep the centers open

Keep the center of the plants open and prune away any diseased leaves and plants. Water the plants before noon and avoid getting the leaves wet. Apply a fresh layer of much around the rose plants (ROSE DISEASES, 2021).

Fungicides

Sometimes it becomes hard to control fungal diseases without the use of fungicides. This is why you might have to invest in fungicides to get rid of diseases such as rust. Choose a fungicide containing mancozeb, sulfur, or chlorothalonil if you wish to take precautionary measures, but use fungicides that contain ingredients such as propiconazole or myclobutanil if you want to control the spread of any existing diseases. These ingredients do a much better job controlling fungus because they are active ingredients that move into the leaves and are foliar systemic. While you are using fungicides, make sure to be extremely cautious and thoroughly read all the labels and directions. Do not overapply or improperly apply the chemicals (ROSE DISEASES, 2021) (Shires, n.d.).

Botrytis Blight

A. What is it?

Sometimes rose flowers and buds can get infected with a gray-brown-looking fuzzy growth that is caused by a gray mold fungus called Botrytis cinerea. It infects a wide range of plants and can cause a devastating loss for ornamental plants and vegetables. Botrytis thrives in cold, humid weather; it particularly thrives in spring and fall. The fungus can invade almost any part of the plant, but it primarily targets softer tissues like the roses and buds. Weakened or injured tissues caused by wounds or aging are also susceptible to infection. The initial sign of this fungus is water-soaked brown spots that develop into gray fuzzy mold over time. Heavily infected petals may breakdown, get matted, and stick together. The infected canes can also have discolored sunken areas, most commonly known as cankers, and dieback that can extend down to the stem. Thrips can also cause similar damage, so look out for the differences so that you can treat them effectively (ROSE DISEASES, 2021) (Ong, n.d.).

B. How to treat it?

Keep the area clean

Keep the area around the plant clean and free of any fallen flowers and leaves because old decaying leaves could foster diseases (ROSE DISEASES, 2021).

Prune and remove fading flowers

Prune off and dispose of all fading flowers and leaves before they get a chance to host any type of bacteria, fungus, or mold (ROSE DISEASES, 2021).

Provide good circulation

Good air circulation is very necessary for the health of the plants because it helps remove and dry off excess moisture from them (ROSE DISEASES, 2021).

Don't wet the leaves

Avoid wetting the leaves since they can take a long time to dry, and if the leaves don't dry properly, it can promote the growth of fungus and other types of viruses and bacteria (ROSE DISEASES, 2021).

Neem oil

If you need to lean towards chemical control, use fungicides containing neem oil because they are the safest and most applicable for home gardens (ROSE DISEASES, 2021).

Copper fungicides

There are fungicides on the market that can help manage diseases. Fungicides that contain natural ingredients such as potassium bicarbonate can be used as preventative measures to protect against diseases that aren't prevalent. Biological fungicides containing Trichoderma harzianum and Streptomyces lydicus can also provide protection. However, if your plant disease is already developing, then choose fungicides with ingredients such as chlorothalonil, fenhexamid, and fludioxonil. Copper fungicides can also be used on dormant bushes (Ong, n.d.).

Rose Rosette Disease

A. What is it?

The rose rosette disease is an untreatable rose disease that is caused by a virus called rose rosette. The virus is introduced into the plants by a rose leaf curl mite. The mite feeds on the sap of the tender stems and leaves, and even though it causes enough damage to the rose plants as it is, if it is a carrier of the virus, the symptoms get even worse. The symptoms appear typically between 1 to 3 months (ROSE DISEASES, 2021).

Roses that are infected with this virus grow thicker and more succulent stems. The infected stems also have an abnormally high number of thorns which may be green or red in color. Roses that grow on these branches are smaller than normal and may be slightly deformed. Lateral branches also grow excessively from the main branches, which creates symptoms like glyphosate on roses. Flowering is also reduced, and the petals that appear on the roses are distorted and a lot fewer in number. The symptoms of this virus generally become evident during the late spring and early summer and progress during the growing season. Once the rose becomes infected with the virus, the virus continues to move throughout the plant until the entire plant is infected. By the time the symptoms become prominent, the virus may have already spread to the neighboring plants due to the movement of the eriophyid mites. The infected plants don't live a very long life and die within a couple of years (ROSE DISEASES, 2021).

There is one thing that makes it hard to diagnose R.R.V., because its symptoms are similar to that of herbicide injury. If the herbicide makes contact with the foliage, it might show the damage immediately, but sometimes the chemical may store itself in the buds and become prominent as spring approaches. Some herbicides may even cause yellowing or stunting of the leaves and witches' broom. The only thing differentiating herbicide injury from R.R.V. is the excessive thorns and the unusual red pigments in the rose branches (Olson, 2017).

B. How to properly treat Rose Rosette

Remove any infected rose

The wild multiflora roses are very susceptible to rose rosette disease, so any wild plants near your roses should be removed and disposed of. Any infected roses should also be removed and burned or bagged for trash pickup (ROSE DISEASES, 2021).

Remove any roots

Remove any roots that might sprout later and make sure not to leave any infected plant rooted in the garden. This is because the mites may travel to other plants. Also, make sure the rose plants have plenty of space between them and aren't touching each other (ROSE DISEASES, 2021).

Bifenthrin spray

R.R.V. is systemic within the infected rose plants; grafting asymptomatic stems on other plants will transmit the virus. Pruners used on diseased plants also need to be disinfected thoroughly using rubbing alcohol or a diluted bleach solution before you can use them on other plants. This is because the sap is also contaminated with the virus (ROSE DISEASES, 2021).

To reduce the spread of the eriophyid mites on your rose plants, the plants neighboring the infected plant need to be treated with bifenthrin spray every two weeks between the months of April and September. The spray can prevent additional plants from becoming diseased (ROSE DISEASES, 2021).

The mites will die in a few days once they don't have an active host. However, they can still survive on fallen debris, which is why it is critical that you remove all the fallen leaves and other foliage and destroy it before replanting roses in that bed. New research has even confirmed that the virus is present in the roots, so you must remove the root ball of all the infected plants before planting new ones. If you want to avoid infected plants from sprouting again, consider a one- or two-month fallow period before replanting the roses (Olson, 2017).

Rose Mosaic

A. What is it?

There can be several causes for the presence of rose mosaic in your roses, but it is typically caused by viruses such as Apple mosaic, Ringspot virus, and Arabis mosaic. Just like the viruses that cause the disease, the symptoms associated with the rose mosaic virus also vary. Yellow wavy lines, mottles in the leaves, and ring spots will happen on some varieties of roses during the growing season. The symptoms are most evident in the spring. The disease causes an overall decrease in the plant quality and infected plants become weaker and more sensitive to damage caused by other stressors like droughts or lower temperatures (ROSE DISEASES, 2021).

B. How to treat Rose Mosaic?

Remove any infected rose

Once the virus infects the plant, it cannot be saved. Rose mosaic spreads super slowly and is established through rose planting that happens through root grafts. This is why you need to remove, bag, and dispose of all the infected parts (ROSE DISEASES, 2021).

Avoid plants with symptoms

Only buy plants from reputable dealers, and particularly avoid purchasing plants that are showing mosaic symptoms (ROSE DISEASES, 2021).

Crown Gall

A. What is it?

The disease is caused by a soil-inhabiting bacteria known as Agrobacterium tumefaciens which often infects ornamental plants. The bacteria cause rounded galls or swelling that occur at or just below the soil surface of the stem or roots. Figuring out this disease just from galls might be a bit difficult since galls appear at pruning sites. The disease can cause weakness, stunting, dieback of shoots, discoloration of leaves, increased susceptibility to winter injury or secondary infection, and finally, wilting and eventually death due to severe infections (ROSE DISEASES, 2021).

B. How to treat it?

Avoid buying infected plants

The first thing you can do to prevent your plants from catching this disease is obviously to avoid buying infected roses in the first place (ROSE DISEASES, 2021).

This disease can't be treated

Once your plants are infected, you can do nothing to get rid of the disease since there is no chemical control for crown gall. All you can do is avoid injuring the crown or roots of the plant during planting or cultivation because the bacteria enter through fresh wounds (ROSE DISEASES, 2021).

Remove and discard soil from the infected plants

Remove the infected plants as soon as you notice galls and if possible, remove and discard any of the soil that was surrounding and encapsulating the infected plant (ROSE DISEASES, 2021).

Disinfect all the tools used

Disinfect all the cutting and pruning tools because the disease can stay on the pruning blades. To disinfect, dip the pruning shears in a solution of 0.5 percent sodium hypochlorite for several minutes (ROSE DISEASES, 2021).

PESTS

Roses are common for homeowners; after all, they are stunning and require little care after they are fully established. And because they are low maintenance, people think that they won't be affected by pests; while there are plenty of rose varieties that are resistant to common rose diseases, there are no varieties that are completely resistant to insect pests. Even low-maintenance roses struggle with rose pests and recognizing them is essential because every pest requires different treatment and control. So, here are a few common pests rose plants struggle with.

1. Aphids

Aphids are pests that have over a hundred different species across North America. They can be found from coast to coast, in every climate, and can also be found on most continents. They are tiny, soft-bodied, and pear-shaped and are about 1/8 of an inch long. They can be red, gray, black, green, yellow, and brown. Some species of aphids have winged forms, and others do not, so treatment will also depend on what kind of aphids you are interacting with since winged aphids would require you to quarantine and treat the neighboring plants as well as the infected plant. In addition, there are small and tube-like structures at the hind end of the aphids, which are known as cornicles (Walliser, n.d.).

There are many plants that are affected by aphids, but roses are among the most susceptible. The pests damage the roses by feeding on the leaves, buds, and the stem; they use their needle-like mouth to pierce the plant tissue and suck at the sap. They feed in a group on newer plant growth or on the underside of the leaves, which causes the leaves, stems, and buds to distort and curl up (Walliser, n.d.).

It is always better to provide your roses with natural control before using chemical control methods because the fewer chemicals your plants have, the better it is for their long-term health. Most of the time, aphids are taken care of by the beneficial insects that live near or on your plants, but if they aren't going away, you can knock them to the ground by a sharp stream of water. You can also use a mixture of 1 tablespoon of soap with 1 liter of water and spray the plant with this mixture over a period of several days. If the organic methods don't work, you can use pesticides such as neem, which inhibits egg-laying, preventing progeny. It is better if you use neem oil as early as possible. And if there is a very extreme infestation case, you can turn to chemical pesticides and use the chemicals according to the instructions provided on the back of the bottle (Fighting against aphids on roses: The best methods, n.d.).

2. Rose Sawflies

If you find large holes in your leaves or find them completely skeletonized, your plants might be infested with a pest most commonly known as rose sawflies. These pests are tiny green caterpillar-like larvae that are only 1/8 to 3/4 of an inch tall. They have light brown heads and are also known as rose slugs. But even though they are called slugs and caterpillars, they are neither, as they are the larva of a type of fly. Sawflies are often found on the underside of leaves, and because they are so small when they are first born, they can be quite difficult to spot (Walliser, n.d.).

If your plants are infested with sawflies, you might need to hand squish them to get rid of the infestation; however, it takes a lot of time. You could try companion planting to discourage the infestation in the first place by pairing your roses with wallflowers, cosmos, dill, alyssum, and fennel. These plants attract parasitic wasps, tachinid flies, and other kinds of beneficial bacteria to control the sawflies naturally. Similar to aphids, you can also try to knock the sawflies off your roses using a sharp stream of water from a hose. While they will still be on your soil, other insects and birds will quickly spot them and eat them up. If none of these control methods work, you might have to turn to insecticides. Choose an insecticide with active ingredients like carbaryl, pyrethrin, or neem oil. All three ingredients have the power to instantly kill bugs when coming into contact with them. The problem with using insecticides is that they don't know good pests from the bad, which is why they often end up killing a lot of beneficial bacteria and pests that are needed to protect the plant (Beaulieu, 2022).

3. Thrips

Rose thrips, also known as western flower thrips, are incredibly tiny, only about 1/20 of an inch. They are slender and brown to yellow in color, and they cause flowers to become streaked with brown or distorted in shape. They feed by sucking out the cells, leaving a sliver streaking behind after feeding. It is very difficult for home gardeners or any kind of grower when thrips attack because they are exceptionally hard to control. They can be worse in landscapes where roses are planted in large numbers. Since they feed on rose buds and the leaves, controlling them can be tricky. To check for an infestation, shake your rose buds over a piece of white paper and look for the insects. If they are hiding inside buds, cut into the infested bud to check for the pests (Walliser, n.d.).

Systemic use of insecticide is the most effective way to get rid of thrips. These insecticides move through the rose bushes, which is why they can catch and kill any pests that are hiding in the plants. Use Spinosad-based organic insecticides, but you can also use neem oil-based products since they are effective and can work for multiple types of pests. If you don't want to go the insecticide route, you can control thrips using beneficial bacteria and pests like lacewings and pirate bugs. If these don't exist naturally in your plants, you can buy them at a local insectary and release them on your roses (Walliser, n.d.) (Griep, Thrips on Roses: How to Kill Thrips in Your Rose Garden, 2020).

4. Slugs

Slugs chew ragged-edged and random-looking holes in the leaves of rose plants. They cause the most damage during the wet growing season and leave slime trails wherever they travel. So, if you see slime trails and holes in the edges or middle of the leaves, then you just might be experiencing a slug infestation. To confirm the infestation, check the rose bushes during the night because they are most active during that time. The rose slug is usually velvety green or yellow green in color, but it can also be light green with stout bristles (Peirce, 2006) (Walliser, n.d.).

To naturally control the slugs, you can encourage birds, toads, frogs, snakes, salamanders, and even ground beetles to make a home in your garden because these animals feed on slugs. You could also twist a copper strip at the bottom of the rose plant so that when the slugs touch it or pass over it, they get a mild shock. If you are unable to naturally control the population of slugs, you could choose to invest in oil sprays. Spray as soon as roses produce full leaves since larvae hatch in the soil and climb up to the leaves (Peirce, 2006).

5. Beetle

Japanese beetle grubs feed on the roots of plants, but adult beetles can use over 300 species of plants as meals, and rose plants are one of them. These pests cause the most problems east of Mississippi, but recently, these beetles have been causing problems in the west as well, and their range has been steadily increasing over the years. They feed on the plant during the day, and because of their size and appearance, they are unmistakable. Japanese beetles are copper-colored and have a green heads. When they are in a defensive position, they raise their rear legs, and while feeding, they release a pheromone that attracts more beetles which is why early and steady control is essential (Walliser, n.d.).

You can handpick the beetles off the plant and drop them in a jar full of soapy water. You could also cover the rose plants with a layer of floating row covers or tulle for a week after you spot the first beetle. Japanese beetles are only active for 4 to 5 weeks, so temporarily covering the plant could prevent most of the damage. You could also spray an organic spray containing Spinosad on the plants because that is the most effective against beetles. Never spray this while pollinators are active, and use such products with great caution (Walliser, n.d.).

6. Spider Mites

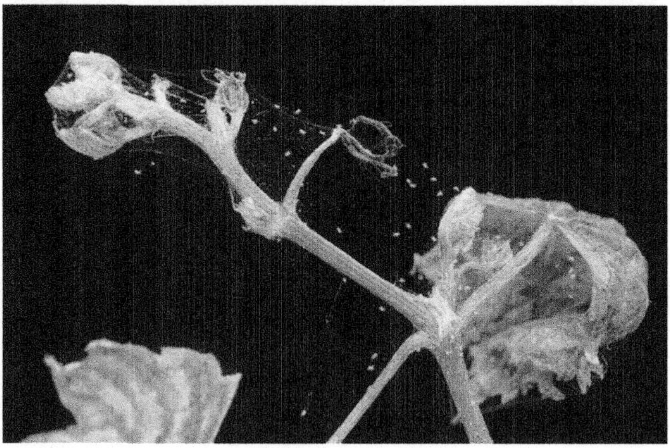

THESE TINY ROSE pests are often incredibly difficult to spot, but the damage they cause to plants is very distinct. They are found all across North America and on a couple of other continents. Because they are only about 1/20 of an inch, you need a magnifying glass or a hand lens to confirm the infestation. The spiders are eight-legged and spin a fine webbing as shelter. The webbing can be easily spotted on the roses, particularly on the underside of the leaves or between the stems. If you suspect that you might have spider mites, you can shake the rose or tap the branch over white paper and look for tiny crawling specks. The spider mites turn the foliage into a mottled, yellow mess (Walliser, n.d.).

Once you have confirmed a spider mite infestation, your best bet is to depend on beneficial pests to control it. Spider mites are a favorite of ladybugs, minute pirate bugs, and big-eyed bugs. Some chemical pesticides can actually encourage mite reproduction; try to avoid them completely. If they get completely out of control, use horticultural oil and insecticide soap since both of them are very effective after two to three applications. One thing you should always avoid is applying insecticides or miticides during the heat of the day. Try to apply them in cooler times like the morning or evening. You should also make sure that your plants are well-hydrated before the applications because watered plants have a much lower chance of having adverse reactions to pesticides (Griep, Getting Rid Of Spider Mites On Roses, 2021) (Walliser, n.d.).

7. Rose Scale

Rose scales look like tiny white or gray bumps along the stem, and because of their appearance, they are often confused with fungus or mold. Rose scale is an immobile, sap-sucking insect that has a very thick shell. After they become adults, these insects spend all their life in one spot, sucking the sap out of plants. When the population of these pests increases, the plants can experience a gradual decline, decreased flowering, and stem and twig dieback.

Heavy infestations can quickly kill your rose bush. These pests are hard to control because their thick shells protect them from most kinds of pesticides (CONNOLLY, 2022).

Rose scale is vulnerable about 4 weeks after they hatch because, at that time, their bodies are soft and have yet to form that hard shell-like coating. A properly timed application of horticultural oil suffocates them at the crawling state. However, if the pests have already developed, removal might be the best way to deal with them. Simply cut off any infested stems and dispose of them (Walliser, n.d.) (CONNOLLY, 2022).

8. Rose Cane Borers

This is another rose pest, but unlike the rest on this list, these don't cause nearly as much damage. They generally cause wilted canes and yellowing foliage, and occasionally, they can kill canes. Rose cane borers tunnel into the cane after it has been pruned. You can spot them if you see a hole at the end of a pruned cane. Depending on where you live, there can be a few different insects that can bore into your roses, but the same treatment can be used (Walliser, n.d.).

If rose cane borers kill a cane, all you need to do is cut off the damaged cane and toss it away. One thing you can do to prevent borers from occurring in the first place is seal the end of the canes with a dab of glue. The glue itself won't harm the plant, but it will make the cane uninhabitable for female wasps (Engel, n.d.) (Walliser, n.d.).

In this chapter, we primarily focused on the different kinds of pests and diseases that plague rose plants. In the next chapter, we will be discussing the last step of the F.L.O.W.E.R.S. method-studying the tips.

CHAPTER 8
STUDY THE ULTIMATE TIPS OF ROSES

~

"When love first came to Earth, the Spring spread rose-beds to receive him."

— THOMAS CAMPBELL

~

Arthur Conan Doyle states, "What a lovely thing a rose is!" because he figured out that aside from beauty, roses can bring humans something that is completely intangible, and that is peace and comfort. In this book, we have covered almost all there is to know about roses and their gardening practices. So, in this last chapter, we will be covering the final step, studying effective tips that will give you more information that might not have made it into the rest of the book. After you are done learning these tips and tricks, you can finally try out whatever you have learned and practice it.

ROSE TIPS

Tip #1: Bare Root Roses Can Be Planted Between November and March

Planting bare-root roses during the dormant winter season is much cheaper than planting container roses because the plants don't need water and additional nutrition when they are dormant. Not to mention, they take up a lot less space and weigh much less when they are being shipped. Additionally, there is a much bigger selection of bare root roses available on the market as compared to container roses, which means you have more choices when picking out the perfect roses for your garden. Bare root roses can be planted at any time between November and the end of March, but if you plant them in autumn, you might be able to get them established much quicker since the soil is still warm from the summer, and moist (Magazine, how to grow roses, 2022).

Tip #2: Roses Are Quite Hungry Plants

Roses are very hungry plants and should be fed regularly throughout the growing season to ensure maximum blooms and growth. From first-year plants to 50-year-old plants, all of them need regular feeding. It is recommended that you use a good nitrogen-rich feed and feed the plants after the late winter pruning, typically done during February. Continue feeding the plants every two weeks throughout the flowering period with potassium-rich feed. Plants that get regularly fed are much bigger, healthier, and are often full of blooms (team, 2020).

Aside from food, roses also require regular watering, especially during the summer. It is very hard to overwater roses; however, they don't like sitting in puddles of cold water. Roses grown in pots should be given water daily throughout the growing season. Newly planted roses also need regular watering until they are fully established (team, 2020).

Tip #3: Use Rose Feed to Promote Summer Flowering

You can buy rose feed that is high in phosphorus to promote summer or repeated flowering of rose plants. You can easily find a bag of rose feed at any gardening store; if you are looking for something more organic, then you can try creating your own phosphorus-rich supplement from banana peels. You need to take two or three banana peels per rose weekly to give your flowers an adequate amount of phosphorus. You can make the supplements in two ways. For the first method, chop up your peels and bury them underneath the rose. Choose an area that has fallen leaves but avoid touching the stem. Dig carefully, avoid touching the roots, and deposit the peels about four inches deep to ward off any critters. For the second method, blend the peels together in a blender, adding the appropriate amount of water. Allow the solution to steep for about 15 minutes. Apply to the soil directly underneath the rose. Toss away any solid residue in your compost (Rose Gardening: Secrets To Success, n.d.).

Tip #4: Don't Forget to Prune Your Roses

Pruning is essential for the overall health, appearance, and vitality of your rose. The best time to cut back your roses is during the summer, immediately after flowering. This is the case for almost all types of roses, except rambling roses. The basic principle of pruning is always the same: cutting back hard will promote the strongest growth, while light pruning will help the plants grow with less vigor. Another basic rule includes cutting towards an outward-facing bud to prevent compacted growth; removing stems that are closely positioned together will help the plant grow more effectively since it will prevent the stems from rubbing against one another. Also, remove short, dead parts of the stem that don't have any growth on them. Remove any twig-looking stems since they are unlikely to produce anything worthwhile both in terms of flowering and growth (Magazine, how to grow roses, 2022).

Tip #5: Don't Waterlog the Soil, but Keep It Moist

Irrigate roses deeply but do it infrequently. Apply direct water to the soil using a soaker hose or a drip irrigation method. Water needs of roses vary depending on the weather, soil, and region, so check the soil before with your finger. Water it often enough, so the soil stays moist, neither soaking wet nor bone dry. To prevent diseases, make sure to keep your foliage dry (Rose Gardening: Secrets to Success, n.d.).

Before picking a spot, ensure it has an adequate amount of drainage because the soil needs to be able to distribute water evenly so that the roots don't sit in puddles of water for long periods. Roses that are directly planted in the ground don't have issues with overly moist soils too often. However, if you are planting your roses in a container, make sure that it has a well-draining hole because if you overwater the soil, it will not be able to distribute it.

. . .

Tip #6: Check Your Roses Frequently

Even though roses are plants that don't require a lot of hands-on work, it is still essential to keep an eye on their progress. This is because the weather can quickly change, and your roses might need more or less water, depending on their condition. It is also very important to catch any rose disease early so that you don't lose any crop. So, even if your roses are doing great at the start of the season, check on them at least twice a week to make sure that they are growing nicely.

Tip #7: Roses Love Rich and Moist Soil

We all know that roses love sunlight, but when they are kept under the burning sun for long periods of time, the soil tends to dry out. You need to start mulching so that you can preserve the water in the soil for as long as possible. Add a 2-to-3-inch layer or a coarse organic mulch around the base of the roses. It should be close to the stem, but it shouldn't touch it because overly moist soils can cause rot or fungus to form on the plant. Coarse mulch helps in reducing foliage diseases on roses by reducing the amount of water splashing on the leaves (Rose Gardening: Secrets to Success, n.d.).

Tip #8: With the First Sight of Blackspot, Treat It Immediately

We have already discussed diseases like black spots and rust in detail in the last chapter. Through that, we know that if these diseases are left to fester, they will not only take over the plant but quickly spread to neighboring plants, destroying everything. This is why you need to be exceptionally vigilant when dealing with plant diseases, particularly in roses, because despite how hardy they seem, they can be surprisingly vulnerable to the slightest things. At the first sign of blackspot, treat it right away and remove the diseased parts from the roses, and burn it so that there is no chance of it coming back (Hawkins, 2014).

Tip #9: Most Roses Will Thrive and Flourish in the Sun

We all know that the secret to growing roses is giving them ample sunlight. They need at least a full six hours of sunlight to grow properly, and if they aren't provided with that, they either don't produce as many roses or the roses they do produce end up being small and visually unappealing. So, if you want strong, stunning roses, plant them in a place that gets plenty of sunlight. And if you are unable to find a place like that in your garden, consider planting inside a container so that you can move the plant around (Hawkins, 2014).

Tip #10: Learn How to Train Climbers

Climbing roses are the perfect plants if you are looking to add height to your garden without being too vigorous. Climbing roses are available in all popular rose varieties, such as hybrid tea roses, English roses, and bourbons. You can even choose plants that produce double or single flowers, are thornless, or scented. Climbing roses can be grown up the house walls, around garden fences, up large obelisks, and over pergolas (Magazine, how to grow roses, 2022).

When you are trying to train your roses, you need to create a system in which you have three main arches growing in all directions, and from them grow the side branches that eventually bear the flowers. Train your main arches to grow at 45 degrees and horizontally, and the side shoots to be as upright as possible. Tie the branches so they are as horizontal as possible without damaging the side branches. If you don't want to do any radial cutting out of season, wait for autumn to properly prune your roses, and in the meantime, try to train them so that they start growing in a pattern, such as a strong horizontal pattern, and cut away anything that doesn't follow it (Magazine, 2019).

Tip #11: Deadhead Your Rose Bushes

Deadheading is often known as the removal of finished or finishing blooms in order to encourage further blooms or growth and also improve the overall shape and appearance of the rose. You should deadhead both repeated flowering shrubs and once flowering shrubs because they don't produce rose hips. However, don't deadhead roses that produce rose hips if you want them in the winter/autumn (What is deadheading?, n.d.).

There are two kinds of deadheading. The first is mainly for aesthetic appeal, removing the browning finished blooms so that you can enjoy the remaining blooming flowers. The second kind encourages the growth of newer blooms and helps maintain shape. To do the first kind of deadheading, you pinch and cut off the finished flower, just underneath the base of where the flower joins the stem. Leave any remaining buds to continue blooming. To do the second kind of deadheading, you need to remove the entire flowering head by cutting the stem just above the first leaf with five leaflets. Once all the flowering heads are removed, cut and dispose of any disproportionally tall stems so that they match the height of the rest of the plant. Try to create a nice round shape as you go about the cutting (What is deadheading?, n.d.).

LEAVE A REVIEW

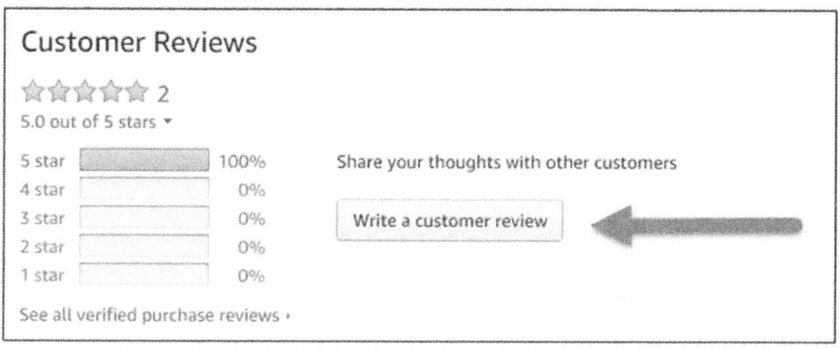

Leave a 1-click review!

I would be incredibly grateful if you take just 60 seconds to write a brief review on Amazon, even if it's just a few sentences.

https://www.amazon.com/review/create-review/?ie=UTF8&channel=glance-detail&asin=1777833760

AFTERWORD

After reading this book, you are probably certain about one thing, and that is the importance of roses in today's society. Even after thousands of years, roses have still maintained their popularity among the masses and people still gravitate towards roses when they are trying to express their love for each other. No one can really fault them; after all, roses are absolutely stunning. Another thing I am sure that you understand is just how easy it is to grow a rose, despite it seeming like a difficult task.

When you are growing plants, experience isn't the most important thing; what is important is the ability to experiment and drive to try again if you fail the first time. Nothing in life is easy, but everything can be achieved with a little effort and education, and that is exactly what I intended to do when I introduced you to the F.L.O.W.E.R.S. method in this book. The first step of the F.L.O.W.E.R.S. method focuses on finding the right rose for your garden. The selection of the rose is the most important part of making sure it thrives in your specific garden. Aside from picking the color and the height of the rose, you will have to consider the size of your garden as well as your purpose for growing roses in the first place. We all live in different regions, so roses that might work for one person won't necessarily work for other people, so make sure to figure out the climate and if it is suitable for growing roses in the first place. This is because roses are sun-loving plants, and they might not thrive in colder regions that don't get as much sunlight. This doesn't mean you should give up on growing roses; always remember that there are many rose varieties, and some of them thrive in colder regions and can even function with less sunlight. This is precisely why the selection of roses is the most important part. The most important things to consider while looking for the perfect rose are hardiness, bloom type, growth habit, and the care requirements.

The second step of the F.L.O.W.E.R.S. method focuses on figuring out the lay of the land. Picking the right spot is just as important as the kind of rose, so keep that in mind while trying to find the perfect place to plant your roses. As I previously mentioned, roses love sunlight, and they need at least a full six hours of sunlight to grow properly, so a sun-filled location is essential. Not to mention, sunlight is a great tool to help fight off any diseases. The next thing you need to consider is space because roses need an ample amount of space to grow; they won't be able to thrive in crowded areas simply because the rubbing of branches can cause an injury that can make the plant vulnerable to pests and diseases. Before settling for a spot, you need to figure out the pH of your soil and if your soil is even healthy enough to support the growth of a rose because roses don't do well in soils that don't drain well. If your soil is okay, but your pH isn't ideal, then there is no need to worry because that can be easily fixed if you add some amendments or organic compost. The amendments will be different depending on what is missing in your soil. Some people hesitate to grow roses because they don't have a backyard, and while that is a valid concern, it can be easily fixed because you can grow in containers or invest in a raised bed. In fact, many people prefer container gardening because their garden soil isn't the best for growing roses, and you can control the quality of the soil if you choose container over in-ground gardening.

The third step discusses the best time to plant roses, and that depends on your zone, the season, and the warmth of the soil. Roses thrive when they are planted in spring or fall, and if you plant them early, you will give them time to root properly. The third step also focuses heavily on companion planting, particularly how you should choose companions for your roses and what plants work best. The fourth step puts special focus on the watering needs of the roses and talks about watering tips all rose gardeners should be aware of. Step four also talks about propagation and how exactly you can multiply your roses. Fertilization and amendment techniques are essential to learning because plant care continues far beyond the actual plantation of the rose, and both are also discussed in detail in this step.

Pruning is essential for the health, flowering, and overall aesthetics of your rose plant, and therefore step five focuses on this subject. Pruning can be pretty tricky, especially for people who have no clue what it is and why it is important, which is why I delve deep into the topic. The sixth step focuses on the common pests and diseases that rose plants might experience. Not only that, but we also discussed how to recognize different diseases and pests, as well as their treatments. The earlier you figure out the problem, the easier it is to tackle because most pests and diseases don't stay contained to one plant and can quickly spread all around your garden. The last step focuses on studying the different rose tips that might be beneficial for you if you are a rose beginner or new to gardening in general.

We discussed a lot in this book, and frankly, even for an experienced gardener, all this information would be intimidating, but there are plenty of people who managed to create stunning rose gardens all on their own. There are many amazing rose gardens around the world that can serve as inspiration, but the biggest one exists in central Japan. It has over 7000 rose varieties. The Park is so beautiful that there is a festival held each year in its honor. When we see such stunning roses around the world, we realize that growing roses goes beyond normal gardening. In fact, many consider it an art, and if you follow the F.L.O.W.E.R.S. method, you too can succeed in becoming an artist that expresses through roses. And you can recreate the best rose gardens right in your backyard.

It is sad to say, but you have reached the end of the book. Please write a review to let us know how your personal rose garden is turning out. Thank you, and good luck with growing!

Also by Stephanie Stephenson

My Book

My Book

FREE GIFT TO OUR READERS

In this Secret You Have in Your Home, you'll learn...

- How to make your garden flourish with ease
- How to control pests and weeds naturally
- Get sweeter tomatoes
- Treating fungus and mildew

Follow the link below to download your free guide.
https://stephaniestephenson.activehosted.com/f/1

BONUS

Join my Facebook Group where I talk about all things gardening and get a free copy of my Garden Planner.

https://www.facebook.com/groups/977894766376839

https://www.facebook.com/groups/977894766376839

REFERENCES

4 Benefits of Pruning Your Trees -. (2016, June 19). Integrity Tree Care. https://www.integritytreecare.org/4-benefits-of-pruning-your-trees/

6 Fascinating Facts About Roses That You Probably Didn't Know. (2022, June 29). Better Homes & Gardens. https://www.bhg.com/gardening/flowers/roses/rose-facts/

10 Fascinating Facts About Roses That Will Simply Astonish You. (n.d.). The Smell of Roses. https://thesmellofroses.com/posts/10-fascinating-facts-about-roses-that-will-simply-astonish-you

A. (2021, January 13). *Benefits of Growing a Rose Garden*. Stanler Farms. https://www.stanlerfarms.co.za/benefits-of-growing-a-rose-garden/

a Href=/Authors/Anne-Balogh.Html>Anne Balogh; Last Updated 9/2/20. (2022, May 20). *Caring for Roses: A Beginner's Rose Growing Guide*. GardenDesign.Com. https://www.gardendesign.com/roses/care.html

Advantages of Roses. (n.d.). eHow. https://www.ehow.com/info_7755741_advantages-roses.html

Austin, M. (2021, April 10). *8 Steps for Choosing the Right Roses for Your Garden*. Just Web World. https://www.justwebworld.com/steps-for-choosing-the-right-roses-for-your-garden/

The Basics of Companion Planting Garden Crops. (2021, November 29). The Spruce. https://www.thespruce.com/companion-planting-with-chart-5025124

BBC Gardeners' World Magazine. (2022, July 15). *How to grow roses*. https://www.gardenersworld.com/how-to/grow-plants/how-to-grow-roses/

The Benefits of Pruning. (2019, January 22). The Grounds Guys. https://www.groundsguys.com/blog/2017/september/the-importance-of-pruning-protect-your-plants-an/

The Best Garden Soil for Growing Roses. (2021a, July 14). The Spruce. https://www.thespruce.com/soil-for-roses-1403048

The Best Garden Soil for Growing Roses. (2021b, July 14). The Spruce. https://www.thespruce.com/soil-for-roses-1403048

Best Garden Soil To Buy For Your Plants. (n.d.). Kellog Garden. https://www.kellogggarden.com/blog/soil/best-garden-soil-to-buy-for-your-plants/

Black Spot Disease of Roses. (n.d.). University of Maryland Extension. https://extension.umd.edu/resource/black-spot-disease-roses

Communications, I. (n.d.). *Container Gardening - UF/IFAS Extension*. (C)Copyright 2017, UF/IFAS. https://sfyl.ifas.ufl.edu/lawn-and-garden/container-gardening/

Connolly, A. (2022, July 8). *Rose Scale: What is It and What to Do About It?* Bustling Nest. https://bustlingnest.com/rose-scale/

Container Gardening. (2017, June 1). Celebrate Urban Birds. https://celebrateurbanbirds.org/learn/gardening/container-gardening/

REFERENCES

Doubrava, N., Blake, J. H., & Williamson, J. (2022, July 20). *Rose Diseases | Home & Garden Information Center*. Home & Garden Information Center | Clemson University, South Carolina. https://hgic.clemson.edu/factsheet/rose-diseases/

Drinkard, R. (2015, November 30). *Stem Canker of Rose*. Ugaurbanag. https://ugaurbanag.com/stem-canker-of-rose/

EFFECTS OF PRUNING ON GROWTH AND SIZE OF TREES. (n.d.). Actahort. https://www.actahort.org/books/146/146_25.htm

Engel, H. (2020, September 21). *Cane Borers & Roses*. Home Guides | SF Gate. https://homeguides.sfgate.com/cane-borers-roses-24472.html

Fighting Against Aphids on Roses. (n.d.). Gardena. https://www.gardena.com/int/garden-life/garden-magazine/fighting-against-aphids-on-roses-the-best-methods/

Great Companion Plants for Roses. (2020, September 17). The Spruce. https://www.thespruce.com/companion-planting-for-roses-1403041

Growing Roses from Cuttings. (n.d.). Garden Tech. https://www.gardentech.-com/blog/how-to-guides/growing-roses-from-cuttings

Grunert, J., More, R., & More, R. (2018, June 21). *When Is the Best Time to Plant Roses?* LoveToKnow. https://garden.lovetoknow.com/wiki/When_Is_the_Best_Time_to_-Plant_Roses

Hagen, L. (2022, June 23). *How to Prune Roses in 8 Simple Steps*. GardenDesign.Com. https://www.gardendesign.com/roses/pruning.html

Healthy Soils. (n.d.). Food and Agriculture Organization of the United Nations. https://www.fao.org/soils-2015/news/news-detail/en/c/277682/

The History of Roses - Our Rose Garden - University of Illinois Extension. (n.d.). Extension Illinois. https://web.extension.illinois.edu/roses/history.cfm

How and When to Mulch Roses. (n.d.). Dummies. https://www.dummies.com/article/home-auto-hobbies/garden-green-living/gardening/general-gardening/how-and-when-to-mulch-roses-180822/

How to Fertilize Roses for Beautiful Bushes. (2022, June 14). The Spruce. https://www.thespruce.com/how-when-to-fertilize-roses-4942489

How to Keep Rose Slugs From Ruining Your Rose Bushes. (2022, February 2). The Spruce. https://www.thespruce.com/rose-sawfly-management-removal-tips-5211557

How to Plant Roses. (2021, January 14). The Spruce. https://www.thespruce.com/how-to-plant-roses-1403055

Iseli, M. (2021, August 13). *Here's How to Protect Your Roses from Bugs — For Good!* Plantophiles. https://plantophiles.com/plant-care/how-to-protect-roses-from-bugs/

J. (2012, November 15). *Symbolism and Meaning of Roses*. Harlow Gardens. https://harlowgardens.com/symbolism-and-meaning-of-roses/

Jackson & Perkins. (n.d.). *how-to-propagate-roses*. Jackson and Perkins. https://www.-jacksonandperkins.com/how-to-propagate-roses/a/how-to-propagate-roses/

K. (2020, January 14). *Rose Soil Guide: Preparing Your Soil for Planting Rose Bushes*. Garden Lovers Club. https://www.gardenloversclub.com/ornamental/flowers/roses/best-soil-for-roses/

K. (2022, May 4). *How Roses Became The Most Popular Flower in History*. Gardenstead.

https://www.gardenstead.com/how-roses-became-the-most-popular-flower-in-history/

Lauren's Garden Service. (2012, February 3). *Choosing Your Garden Location.* Landscape Design, Installation, Maintenance and Native Plant Nursery | Lauren's Garden Service. https://www.laurensgardenservice.com/gardening-tips/choosing-your-garden-location/

Lett, S. (2022, June 8). *How to Mulch Your Roses.* David Austin Roses - EU. https://eu.davidaustinroses.com/blogs/news/how-to-mulch-your-roses

Location to Grow Roses. (n.d.). Gardening Know How. https://www.gardeningknowhow.-com/ornamental/flowers/roses/location-to-grow-roses.htm

Lofgren, K. (2022, July 9). *How to Choose the Best Location to Grow Roses in Your Yard.* Gardener's Path. https://gardenerspath.com/plants/flowers/best-rose-location/

Loughrey, P. W. G. J. (2022a, February 18). *Guide to Fertilizing Roses: When & How to Fertilize.* GardenDesign.Com. https://www.gardendesign.com/roses/fertilizer.html

Loughrey, P. W. G. J. (2022b, February 25). *The 12 Best Types of Roses for Your Garden.* GardenDesign.Com. https://www.gardendesign.com/roses/types.html

M. (2015, October 5). *10 top tips for growing healthy roses.* Woman's Weekly. https://www.womansweekly.com/gardening/10-top-tips-growing-healthy-roses-14533/

Menon, P. (2022, May 10). *10 Amazing Health Benefits of Rose Flower.* Krishijagran. https://krishijagran.com/health-lifestyle/10-amazing-health-benefits-of-rose-flower/

Moulton, M. (2022, February 16). *12 Rose Companion Plants (& What Not To Grow Near Roses).* Blooming Backyard. https://www.bloomingbackyard.com/rose-companion-plants/

Peirce, P. (2012, January 15). *Oil spray is best bet for combatting rose slug.* SFGATE. https://www.sfgate.com/homeandgarden/goldengategardener/article/Oil-spray-is-best-bet-for-combatting-rose-slug-2532164.php

Planet Natural. (2018a, May 4). *How to Propagate Roses.* https://www.planetnatural.-com/rose-gardening-guru/propagating/

Planet Natural. (2018b, May 4). *How to Propagate Roses.* https://www.planetnatural.-com/rose-gardening-guru/propagating/

Poindexter, J. (2020a, September 5). *The Pros & Cons of 18 Gardening Methods and Which One is Right for You.* MorningChores. https://morningchores.com/gardening-methods-pros-cons/

Poindexter, J. (2020b, September 5). *The Pros & Cons of 18 Gardening Methods and Which One is Right for You.* MorningChores. https://morningchores.com/gardening-methods-pros-cons/

Popular Rose Cultivars. (n.d.). Masterclass. https://www.masterclass.com/articles/types-of-roses#9-popular-rose-cultivars

Radford, T. (2022, May 25). *How to Plant Roses (with Pictures).* wikiHow. https://www.wikihow.com/Plant-Roses

rose | Description, Species, Images, & Facts. (n.d.). Encyclopedia Britannica. https://www.britannica.com/plant/rose-plant

Rose Diseases. (n.d.). HGIC. https://hgic.clemson.edu/factsheet/rose-diseases/

Rose Gardening: Secrets To Success. (n.d.). Bioadvanced. https://bioadvanced.com/growing-roses-secrets-success

Rose powdery mildew / RHS Gardening. (n.d.). Royal Horticultural Society. https://www.rhs.org.uk/disease/rose-powdery-mildew

Rose Pros And Cons – World of Garden Plants. (2021, December 17). Worldof Garden Plants. https://worldofgardenplants.com/rose-pros-and-cons/

Rose Rosette Disease - Oklahoma State University. (2017, February 1). OKState. https://extension.okstate.edu/fact-sheets/rose-rosette-disease.html

Rose Soil Preparation. (n.d.). Gardening Know How. https://www.gardeningknowhow.-com/ornamental/flowers/roses/rose-soil-preparation.htm

Rose Spider Mites. (n.d.). Gardening Know How. https://www.gardeningknowhow.-com/ornamental/flowers/roses/rose-spider-mites.htm

Roses. (n.d.). Almanac.Com. https://www.almanac.com/plant/roses

Roses Thrips. (n.d.). Gardening Know How. https://www.gardeningknowhow.com/ornamental/flowers/roses/rose-thrips.htm

Soil Preparation. (n.d.). Treloarroses. https://www.treloarroses.com.au/Soil-Preparation

Texas A&M AgriLife Extension Service. (2019a, March 4). *Botrytis Blight of Roses - What causes Botrytis blight?* https://agrilifeextension.tamu.edu/library/landscaping/botrytis-blight-of-roses/

Texas A&M AgriLife Extension Service. (2019b, March 4). *Crown Gall of Roses - What are the symptoms of crown gall?* https://agrilifeextension.tamu.edu/library/landscaping/crown-gall-of-roses/

The Types of Roses and How to Choose a Rose Plant. (n.d.). Hunker. https://www.hunker.-com/13731880/the-types-of-roses-and-how-to-choose-a-rose-plant

Walliser, J. (2020, February 25). *Rose pests and how to control them organically.* Savvy Gardening. https://savvygardening.com/rose-pests/

Watering Roses. (n.d.). Heir Loom Roses. https://www.heirloomroses.com/info/watering-roses

Watering Roses. (2015, June 9). Better Homes & Gardens. https://www.bhg.com/gardening/flowers/roses/watering-roses/

What Is a Raised Bed, Anyway? (2022, August 20). Miraclegro. https://www.miraclegro.-com/en-us/library/raised-bed-gardening/what-raised-bed-anyway

What is Pruning? Importance, Benefits & Methods of Pruning | Davey Blog. (n.d.). Davey. https://blog.davey.com/2018/09/what-is-pruning-the-importance-benefits-and-methods-of-pruning/

The Worlds Largest Rose Garden Flower Festival. (n.d.). Facebook. https://www.facebook.-com/unsupportedbrowser

York, P. S. (2022, July 5). *How To Plant a Rose Bush for Beginners.* Southern Living. https://www.southernliving.com/garden/flowers/how-to-plant-roses

Printed in Great Britain
by Amazon

43335022R00109